A Place of
Encounter

Renewing Worship Spaces

D. Foy Christopherson

Augsburg Fortress

A PLACE OF ENCOUNTER
Renewing Worship Spaces

Editors: Suzanne Burke, Robert Farlee, Jessica Hillstrom
Cover and interior design: Laurie Ingram
Cover photo: Florence, Italy, San Miniato Church; © Andrea Pistolesi/Getty Images

ISBN 0-8066-5107-5

Manufactured in the U.S.A.

07   06   05   2   3   4   5   6   7   8   9   10

For Myrtle Naomi Berg

for her love, faith, and artistry

Contents

Preface

This book is an exploration of the issues raised by the Renewing Worship initiative of the Evangelical Lutheran Church in America (ELCA), specifically the twenty-five principles for worship space and the Christian assembly set forth in the ELCA's *Principles for Worship* (Renewing Worship, vol. 2, pp. 68–74).

This book is not intended to be a process guide for renewing church buildings nor a building project manual. It is not a comprehensive history of church architecture. It is not a renovation guide or architectural handbook. The author hopes it will be a useful resource for (1) committees, small groups, and education programs gathering to learn, perhaps for the first time, about worship space; (2) communities early in the process of considering a new building or renewing an existing space and establishing a common understanding and theological foundation from which to move forward; and (3) anyone wishing to enter into the Renewing Worship initiative and the church's ongoing discussion about worship practice.

The ELCA's statement on the practice of word and sacrament, *The Use of the Means of Grace,* and *Principles for Worship* are foundational documents for this book and would be valuable to have close at hand. Both are available to every reader to access free of charge via the Renewing Worship Web site: www.renewingworship.org.

This book will be of interest to:

- those who are responsible for the day-to-day preparation of existing worship spaces for sacramental celebrations and for the changing themes of the church's year
- those interested in changing or creating worship spaces
- pastors, educators, worship committees, building committees, and altar guilds
- those interested in the church's worship life and its environment

This book is intended to generate discussion and engagement with the Renewing Worship process in local worshiping assemblies. It does not intend to represent or defend the principles, which have been set forth as provisional materials, representing the wisdom of many in the church. The application and background material of the principles may be valuably used as the leader guide when leading a small group through this resource. Reflect on or discuss each principle as it can be applied in your ministry context. The reproducible pages for the formational arts inventory suggested in the text can be found in the appendix. Readers will also find resources for improving, renewing, or creating worship spaces, and a bibliography for further study.

Any good ideas you find in this book were surely inspired by others who deserve thanks and credit: those professors and church leaders at whose feet I've had the privilege to sit, especially in the area of worship and the arts: Walter C. Huffman, James Notebaart, Frank Burch Brown, R. Kevin Seasoltz, Carlton Gross, Gary Reed†, and Paul R. Nelson†; congregations and church leaders who have graciously invited me into their holy places, indulging me in poking and prodding their own places of encounter; and those who wrote the books that formed my love of worship and the arts. Much of the content of this book has been developed over time for workshops and presentations or through participation in various study groups. Most assuredly, ideas included here have come from participants and colleagues in these endeavors who also deserve thanks. Thanks go to Patrick Russell for his helpful comments and to editor Suzanne Burke who was always encouraging. Any shortcomings this book may have are entirely my own.

D. Foy Christopherson
Festival of Pentecost, 2004

1
How Are We Gonna Get This Thing to Serve?

The church has no building code, save proclaiming Christ crucified and risen. No architectural or artistic style is distinctly Lutheran, but some ways of interpreting and bearing witness to the good news of Jesus Christ are.

During the Protestant Reformation Martin Luther maintained many of the arts that other reformers chose to abandon. Luther's worship reforms were made in support neither of the old and traditional nor of the new and innovative, but rather in favor of what may be effective in communicating the gospel clearly and pastorally. Under that judgment, music and musical instruments were maintained. Luther's only architectural comment indicated a desire that the presiding minister be able to face the assembly across the altar-table. Vestments and other textiles were maintained in Lutheran churches, as were sculpture and a variety of architectural styles and features.

Lutherans understand that the arts form and shape faith, whether this influence is intended or not. We also understand that the arts can be tools to proclaim the gospel, supporting the Lutheran impulse to use every available media for that proclamation. Luther's followers were among the first to take advantage of the newly invented printing press, putting it quickly in service to the gospel and establishing the ministry of publishing.

Music is the art form for which Lutherans (and Luther) are known. Much has been written and said about music for Lutheran worship. Lately, the hot topic has been one of style: what type of music shall we use in worship? The ELCA's Renewing Worship project recently published provisional principles for worship dealing with this and three other topics: language for worship, preaching, and worship space. You can find these on the Internet (www.renewing worship.org) or in the publication *Principles for Worship,* Renewing Worship, vol. 2 (ELCA/ Augburg Fortress, 2002). You may find it helpful to keep these principles nearby when reading this book.

Though many of the same questions that musicians have been asking apply to the other arts, these newly developed principles for language, preaching, and worship space are a welcome addition to the conversation. The other arts have not participated in the ongoing conversation from which musicians and theologians have benefited.

In 1959, just as the age of modern church architectural innovation was beginning, Luther D. Reed wrote, "Architecture is in many respects the greatest of the arts in the service of the church. It fashions the fabric which other arts enrich. Within this fabric Christian assemblies worship and work" (*Worship,* p. 10). Forty years later, in the midst of a postmodern, post-Christian, and visual age, it is time to extend our conversations to worship space and the related visual arts in service to the gospel.

No matter your circumstance—sitting around a set of proposed blueprints for your new building, gathered with the altar guild to make plans for preparing the worship environment for an upcoming season, or thinking about how you use your existing space—the question before you is the same: "How are we gonna get this thing to serve?" How are we going to get this building to serve something larger than itself? How can we use the visual arts as a tool for worship, for Christian formation, for evangelism, for mission? That's also where *Principles for Worship,* "Worship Space and the Christian Assembly" begins: describing spaces that serve mission, that serve the assembly and its worship, and that serve justice.

If they're going to serve, our buildings and worship environments have to be places where our communities can meet God. They must be places of encounter. To quote my friend Craig Satterlee, we understand that God has said, in effect, "If you need to find me in a hurry, it's bread, water, wine, word. That's where I'll be." God, of course, can act anywhere else God desires. But when we're in a pinch, we know that God has promised to be in baptism, in holy communion, in the word shared. These places are where we go when we need to find God. They are the places where God is transforming the world today. These places of encounter with the means of grace, these places in our care and under our stewardship, are the places of which we need to ask the question, "How are we gonna get this thing to serve?"

Now, about preparing the environment for this encounter: fire anyone on your committee who thinks the task is to *decorate* the church or to build a monument. Well, firing is a little severe, so let them stay, but guide them into better practice. We don't merely decorate our church buildings. We take the whole project much more seriously than that! These are places of encounter with the living God we're talking about! More than merely decorating, we strive to create art that proclaims the gospel, makes Christ known, and forms lives of faith. That's why we're guided by principles—to help us make theological, pastoral, and aesthetic judgments about places of encounter that are simultaneously permanent and temporary, that are crafted by amateurs and professionals together. We value congregational participation in all aspects of worship, including creating visual arts together.

2
What Is a Church?

There have always been many ideas about what the church should be. Ask the bride, and one answer will emerge. Ask the organist, the choir, or the worship band and you'll get one or two more. Ask a Christian from the Orthodox East, or someone who lives in a residential religious community, a seminary, or retreat center, and the list will grow. A suburban family may have a different answer than an urban woman or a rural man. A weekly worshiper will have a different answer than the atheist passer-by. A Californian will answer differently than a Pennsylvanian. And the Minnesotan may have still a different idea. A Baptist answer will be different from an Episcopalian or Roman Catholic answer. The Roman Empire's answer was different from the medieval answer, and the 1950s and 1960s had a different answer still. The 20-year-old will perhaps answer differently than the 70-year old. And all these answers are important visions of the church.

What is a church? Disagreement is likely about what the question means in the first place. Are you talking about the congregation—the community that assembles there—or are you talking about the building it owns and operates? Yes.

The Renewing Worship project continues to explore the worship dimensions of this question for ELCA Lutherans at the turn of the twenty-first century. Even by narrowing the question to one denomination in one region of the world for one time, we are sure to have diverse answers. The ELCA is marvelously diverse and exciting to witness, which is evident as congregations engage the Renewing Worship project. At the same time, we recognize a strong common unity, which is where we begin: with what unites us, discovering and celebrating the unity within our diversity that holds us together.

The diversity of Lutheran Christians gives rise to diverse needs, tastes, and expectations in buildings that serve us and our ministries. Some groups even reject the idea of a building altogether! How can we ever come to a common understanding about what a church's building is?

Every denomination is unique in what unites it. Communions may be united by history, organizing principle, theology, founder, or by a common worship book. Lutherans around the world are united by common understandings as outlined in documents from the Protestant Reformation of the sixteenth century. Every ELCA pastor (at ordination) and every ELCA congregation (in its constitution) confess "that the Holy Scriptures are the Word of God and are the norm of its faith and life, . . . accept, teach, and confess the Apostles', the Nicene, and the Athanasian Creeds, [and] . . . acknowledge the Lutheran Confessions as true witnesses and faithful expositions of the Holy Scriptures" (*Occasional Services*, p. 194). So when faced with our question, "What is the church?" Lutherans instinctively begin with this foundation. Those documents—the holy scriptures, the creeds, and the confessions—define the church for us.

Living stones

When discussing art and environment for worship, a common biblical phrase used to describe the church is "living stones." 1 Peter 2:5

says, "Like living stones, let yourselves be built into a spiritual house, to be a holy priesthood, to offer spiritual sacrifices acceptable to God through Jesus Christ." Environment and art statements often speak of the assembly in this way. *Principles for Worship* says, "The scriptures speak of the people of God as 'living stones . . . built into a spiritual house.' Gathered to Christ, the cornerstone precious in God's sight, the worshiping assembly is a place where God makes a home" (background S-4A, p. 71). Roman Catholics in the United States made this phrase the title of their new statement on environment and art, *Built of Living Stones* (2000).

The ecumenical creeds (Apostles', Nicene, Athanasian) go on to define the church with adjectives: "one, holy, catholic, and apostolic," a single people united and undivided, set apart, universal, in the tradition of the apostles.

Principles for Worship quotes Hippolytus, an early leader in the church. In the *Apostolic Tradition,* we read: "It is not a place that is called 'church,' nor a house made of stones and earth. . . . What then is the church? It is the holy assembly of those who live in righteousness" (background S-1A, p. 68). Revelation 21:3 reminds us that God's home is with God's people.

The assembly is the church

Finally, the Lutheran confessions, the documents that give identity to Lutherans all over the world, say: "It is also taught that at all times there must be and remain one holy, Christian church. It is the assembly of all believers among whom the gospel is purely preached and the holy sacraments are administered according to the gospel" (Augsburg Confession, *Book of Concord,* p. 42).

Principles for Worship takes time to do a short study on the Greek word for church *ekklesia*—"a biblical word for the church that has at its root the meaning 'called out' "—and then defines the church this way: "The worship of the Christian assembly . . . is at the heart of the church's identity and purpose" (p. vi). The church is further defined by the activities in which the assembly is engaged: "The people of God are called by the Holy Spirit to *gather* around the *word of God* and the *sacraments*, so that the Spirit may in turn *send* them into the world to continue the mission of God" (p. vi).

In the background to Principle S-7, *Principles for Worship* states clearly: "The foundational symbol of the church is the gathered assembly itself, which transcends every barrier, such as class, ethnicity, and age. . . . There is broad ecumenical agreement that the assembly is the starting place in the task of understanding and renewing worship and the place of worship" (p. 75). Much more can be said about the nature of the church, but for our purpose in discussing worship space we have established that the assembly of believers is the church, the group among to whom the gospel is proclaimed and the sacraments are administered, using a pattern of gathering, word, meal, and sending.

Everything begins with the assembly

Everything begins with the assembly. God acts. God gathers a people. God makes a covenant. God creates a community. From the earliest covenant, the people have gathered together to give God thanks for their deliverance, for their ongoing welfare, and to ask for God's presence and protection for their future. God lives not in a temple, or on a mountaintop, but in the midst of the people, with the people, in the assembly.

As a nomadic people, Israel understood God to travel with them, in a pillar of smoke and fire at first. Then God dwelt with them in a tent. As Israel wandered, they came across sites of past deliverance. There they stopped to remember God's saving activity, and to raise up a monument, an *ebenezer*, a pile of stones to remind them that this site was one of deliverance, and hence a holy place.

When Israel entered into the promised land, they became a settled people. No longer encountering their nomadic sites of deliverance, they eventually developed a calendar to celebrate these acts of deliverance in time rather than by returning to the original geography. Now with permanent dwellings of their own, they felt that God should also dwell in a house. After all, other nations had temples for their gods. From that impulse the temple in Jerusalem emerged.

But the temple was problematic: not all of Israel lived in Jerusalem, where the temple was. An annual pilgrimage to the temple, made by many to offer sacrifice to God, was an arduous and expensive journey. And how did they worship in their village if the temple was in Jerusalem? Also, Israel was hauled off to exile twice, and the temple was destroyed twice. So where did God live then? Israel's God was not well-suited to live in a temple. Israel's God was a God of the people. In 2 Samuel 7:5-7 the Lord sends a message to David: "Are you the one to build me a house to live in? I have not lived in a house since the day I brought up the people of Israel from Egypt to this day, but I have been moving about in a tent and a tabernacle. Wherever I have moved about among all the people of Israel, did I ever speak a word with any of the tribal leaders of Israel, whom I commanded to shepherd my people Israel, saying, 'Why have you not built me a house of cedar?' "

As a result of the destruction of the temple during the exiles and the final destruction in A.D. 70 by the Romans, Jewish worship became centered in the home. Domestic Friday night Sabbath celebrations continue to this day.

A further result of the experience of exile or the distance to Jerusalem was the development of the synagogue, a local gathering of at least ten Jewish men for prayer and study. These groups, gatherings of families, eventually acquired leader-teachers, rabbis, and buildings, also called synagogues. It was in these kinds of gatherings that Jesus preached and taught, and it was this kind of community—teacher and disciples—that Jesus gathered around himself. Jesus' group was itinerant, however, and never had a building of its own. Even after his death and resurrection, Jesus' followers attended synagogue, prayed, heard readings from the Law and the Prophets, and heard the rabbi teach from these sacred texts.

The God of Israel, the God of Jesus, lives in the midst of the assembly! That's us!

The assembly is the primary icon of Christ

I once worshiped with a community of Benedictine monks for the Vigil of All Saints (Halloween or All-Hallows Eve). The community gathered first at the baptismal font in the doorway of the chapel to remember God's baptismal covenant promises for us and for all the faithful before us. We were then invited to process two-by-two, following the monks' example, to the front of the chapel to continue the liturgy. Upon arriving at the head of the aisle near the altar, we were to follow the ritual practice of the monks: each pair of monks bowed first to the altar, to reverence the body of Christ in the meal, and then turned and bowed to one another, in the person of their partner in the procession, to reverence the body of Christ in us, before separating to go into the choir stalls. That simple action of honoring the Christ who is in each of us left a powerful and lasting impression on me.

The primary symbol of Jesus in the room is the *people* because the people embody Christ. Paul writes: "Now you are the body of Christ and individually members of it" (1 Cor. 12:27). Teresa of Avila said:

> Christ has no body now on earth but yours;
> No hands but yours;
> No feet but yours;
> Yours are the eyes through which to look out Christ's
>   compassion on the world;
> Yours are the feet with which he is to go about doing good;
> Yours are the hands with which he is to bless folk now!
> —www.prayingchurch.org/teresa.html

Jesus gave us his body so we could become his body. As the body of Christ, the assembly makes Christ present. The assembly is the living symbol of Christ in the world, and in the church. As such, the assembly in the worship space has primary place. Art and architecture that suggest otherwise are misleading. When the fancy floors or fancy walls adorn only the spaces where the leaders sit, we have a problem. Floor plans that suggest that some parts of the worship space are more sacred or more holy than the area where the assembly sits do not serve the assembly. Room arrangements that remove, distance, or separate the assembly from the altar-table, the word proclaimed, or the font, are not helpful. Lighting systems that feature all sorts of flexibility for the leaders and none for the assembly, or buildings that suggest the assembly is an audience at a performance do not respect the assembly as the body of Christ. Seasonal worship environments or holiday "decoration" plans that don't include and adorn the place of the assembly or that impede the assembly's work of worship, witness, and service are incomplete, if not ill-conceived.

The writer of 1 Peter reminds us that the assembly gathers as "a chosen race, a royal priesthood, a holy nation, a purchased people" (1 Peter 2:9). When we ask, "How are we gonna get this thing to serve?" it is the assembly's gathering, its ability to do its work, its liturgy, for the sake of the world, that must be considered. The active presence and participation of the body of Christ is the central thing.

That Halloween with the Benedictines was memorable in another way as a reflection of art and environment. Along the way, the route of that procession brought us up the main aisle and through the midst of pews where the congregation normally assembles. There, for this one night, spread through the empty, darkened pews were small votive lights, many of which were accompanied by one of the community's many reliquaries, representing for them the church of days gone by. This powerful environment, faithful to their tradition and experience, suggested to me in a whole new artistic way the great cloud of witnesses who have gone before us!

Understanding of the assembly in the worship space

The word *assembly* is used frequently in this book and in *Principles for Worship* to describe the worshiping congregation, following the practice of the Augsburg Confession: the church is "the assembly of all believers among whom the gospel is purely preached and the holy sacraments are administered according to the gospel" (Article 7, *The Book of Concord*, p. 42). This word *assembly* appears to be emerging in ecumenical consensus in statements about environment and art, replacing *congregation* when speaking about the worshiping community. The implication is that a congregation is identified primarily as a worshiping community rather than simply as its membership. Richard Giles, speaking of the assembly, says, "In Christian liturgy . . . there is no audience, only participants in the unfolding drama of the saving work of Jesus" (*Re-Pitching the Tent*, p. 44).

Foundation. Principal symbol of faith. Primary icon. Body of Christ. These words express our understanding of assembly and reinforce the critical point that when considering principles for worship space and when shaping those spaces themselves, the assembly itself is the starting point. The assembly is the primary symbol of Christ in our spaces.

What about the cross?

"What about the cross?" you might ask. Isn't the cross the primary symbol of Christ? A cross or crucifix (a cross holding an image of the body of Jesus) is a basic Christian symbol in any liturgical celebration but it is not a place of liturgical action for the purposes of our discussion. We currently understand the cross as the primary visual symbol of our Christian identity and faith, and of our redemption. Its use as a symbol developed relatively late because it was likely too offensive to use when crosses were still active tools of execution, conjuring images of death rather than resurrection life.

Nearly every Christian worship space has a cross. Today many are arguing for a single, dominant cross. A multiplicity of any symbol, crosses included, has the effect over time of diluting its power. This single cross is ideally portable, in order that it can lead, follow, or mark the living symbol of Christ, the assembly, as it goes about its liturgy. Think of the cross in the space as marking or identifying, maybe even branding, the assembly. "Marked with the cross of Christ forever," we are reminded in holy baptism. In that sense it travels with its people, comes and goes with them. It leads us in procession. It can accompany the coffin all the way to the cemetery. (Scheduling crucifers for funerals with a parental release from school allows youth to experience how the faithful meet death apart from any personal experience of grief.) The cross leads us out into the neighborhood on Palm Sunday. Perhaps its place is in the gathering space midweek while the body of Christ is at work in the world. From there it leads the assembly into worship on the Lord's day. However formal or informal your worship practice is, consider how this symbol can serve best.

We have diversity of practice in our choice of cross styles: rugged, precious metals and precious stones, empty, with the body of Christ (corpus) as man of sorrows, with corpus as triumphant risen Lord, as if reigning from a throne. The suggestion that only one cross be used by the assembly at any one time does not prohibit using a variety of crosses throughout the seasons of the year.

A more critical question is one of size. For the cross to be moveable, it needs to be built as a processional cross. The scale of the cross should be carefully considered. To be satisfying, the cross will need to be both big enough to be seen by the assembly and light enough to carry in procession. Though providing the cross might seem a simple design and building project, accomplishing both of these objectives will be difficult for the amateur. The selection of the assembly's cross is one place where congregations might seek out expert advice.

One way to further honor the cross, perhaps as part of a celebration of Holy Cross Day (September 14) or Back to School/Homecoming/Rally Day, would be to invite congregation members to bring in crosses that have personal meaning. Use these crosses to create an "art gallery" of crosses of varying styles in a gathering place or hall. Create gallery cards to identify the source and origin of each cross. A variation is the gallery of nativity sets that are assembled at Christmas in some congregations. Both ideas allow for great congregational participation in creating parish art exhibits.

When selecting any art for worship, education, or formation that contains an image of the crucified and risen Jesus, be sure the artist included the scars from the crucifixion. Images that deny the suffering of the cross do not serve the theology of the cross, honored among Lutherans.

Worship is the primary act of the church

The church's purpose is to "worship God in proclamation of the Word and administration of the sacraments and through lives of prayer, praise, thanksgiving, witness and service" (Constitution, Bylaws, and Continuing Resolutions of the Evangelical Lutheran Church in America, 4.02). Since the times of the early church, "The baptized devoted themselves to the apostles' teaching and fellowship, to the breaking of bread and the prayers" (Acts 2:42).

In worship we rehearse who we should be as Christians. In learning we delve deeper into those things. And in Christian life (witness and service), we actually live out what we have just discovered. Through praise, prayer and proclamation, we are formed by worshiping together. This principle, that communal activity forms us, was characterized well on the sit-com *Designing Women*, when a 102-year-old woman, quoting her grandfather, said:

We ain't what we oughtta be.
We ain't what we're gonna be.
But thank God we sure ain't what we was.

Is it too bold to claim that through Christian worship God is changing the world today, transforming us, week by week, into God's own body, for the sake of the world? We are a work in progress, God's work of redeeming the world. Through word and sacrament, we are being transformed into the leaven that will raise the whole loaf. One bumper sticker in circulation says, "Tired of the world? Try Jesus!" Well, Jesus hasn't given up on this old world. He is deeply present in it. Each Lord's day we are met again by the living God who sends us out to be his hands and feet. That's why "pie in the sky, by and by, when I die" just won't fly. It is in worship, in the liturgy, that we are clothed and fed, encouraged, and sent right back out there again for another week to be God's transforming presence in the world. In worship, justice walks hand in hand with transforming beauty.

This worship has a pattern: gathering, word, meal, sending

Jesus *gathered* his followers around him, *taught* from the holy scriptures, and *broke bread* with them. Remember that first Easter evening, on the road to Emmaus? "Beginning with Moses and all the prophets, Jesus interpreted to [the disciples] the things about himself in all the scriptures. . . . When he was at table with them, he took bread, blessed and broke it, and gave it to them. Then their eyes were opened and they recognized him" (Luke 24:27, 30-31a). This pattern is celebrated weekly. The church assembles on Sunday, the Lord's day, the anniversary of the resurrection, and the day of most of the post-resurrection appearances of Jesus. We gather to see Jesus on this day on which we have seen him in the past.

Principles for Worship is explicit in outlining this pattern of gathering, word, meal, and sending: "The people of God are called by the Holy Spirit to *gather* around the *word of God* and the *sacraments*, so that the Spirit may in turn *send* them into the world to continue the mission of God" (p. vi). Witness (teaching, evangelism) and service (outreach) follow as the other marks of the church. Our buildings are the working out of this theology in bricks and mortar. The Lutheran confessions, churchwide statements on sacramental practice, and ecumenical resources all serve as further guides. (For a fuller discussion of this pattern, or to gather a small group or class around this pattern, see *Gathered and Sent: An Introduction to Worship* in the bibliography.)

This worship is sacramental

Lutherans identify two sacraments: Holy Baptism and Holy Communion. The ELCA's statement on sacramental practice, *The Use of the Means of Grace*, guides our celebration of these central activities. Sacraments, the means of grace, deserve mention in a book about worship environment because of their very nature. Jesus took ordinary bread, wine, and water and united them with extraordinary promises for us. His blessing and attention to these things suggests the power that the natural world can have in bringing the gospel to us. Augustine called them "visible word." It is through participation in these sacraments that we become the body of Christ. Our spaces for worship must be functionally designed to accommodate these sacramental events, to house the activities that bind us together in identity and mission.

These activities, washing in the word and dining in the kingdom of God, generate other activity for mission, formation, and evangelization. The assembly must be able to engage in these activities when it gathers. "How are we gonna get this thing to serve?" First we must be sure that our spaces serve the assembly, the bath, the word, and the meal.

The assembly space includes primary centers for the celebration of the word of God and the sacraments, secondary areas that facilitate the roles of all the leaders, and other spaces that complement the requirements of communal worship. Principle S-7

After the assembly, flowing water, bread, wine, and proclaimed word are the essential elements in the space. We encounter the Lord through baptism, eucharist, and proclamation (application S-18A, p. 89). Furthermore, "Art and architecture proclaim the gospel, enrich the assembly's participation in the word and sacraments, and reinforce the themes of the occasion and season" (principle S-5, p. 72).

Sign and symbol

We often use the words *sign* and *symbol* interchangeably, but in our discussion about worship space let's make a clear distinction. A sign (like a stop sign) has a single, unambiguous and unchanging meaning. It would be a dangerous thing for an eight-sided red sign to have multiple meanings to different drivers. Its meaning has been defined and standardized by the United Nations so that no matter the language of the words on this red eight-sided sign, you know exactly what to do when you see it.

A symbol, on the other hand, has many meanings. It is multivalent. Its meaning can vary with the circumstance, community, time, application, situation in life, and individual. This characteristic is partly what gives symbols their enduring power to communicate deep meanings. Symbols generate discussion, meditation, works of art. Nobody meditates on the meaning of a stop sign. Hardly anyone makes a stop sign the subject of a work of art (Andy Warhol being an exception!). The assembly is a symbol. The cross is a symbol. Water is a symbol. Holy Communion and baptism are symbols whose depth of meaning we cannot exhaust over the course of a lifetime. Symbols are by definition more interesting than signs. They are the tools of artists.

Language occupies a middle ground between sign and symbol. Letters of the alphabet and words are harder to define. Usually words operate as signs, in strictly defined combinations (remember studying your vocabulary words?), representing a single idea, object, or concept. Get too creative with them, rearrange them or draw them differently, and they lose their meanings. Calligraphy is likely the one art form that uses words effectively to create symbols with greater meaning. For those of us who are not calligraphers, sticking letters on a banner that spell "Jesus is born!" makes a sign that doesn't offer much additional symbolic interest. But imagine what a well-crafted image suggesting a homeless newborn might mean to a variety of people. For how long could we meditate upon that? *Alleluia* may be one word that functions more as symbol than sign. What do you think?

An environment free of nonessentials or the duplication of symbols brings clarity to what is central in worship. Principle S-18

One more thought about symbols: The duplication of a symbol usually diminishes its power. Two podiums offer less visual focus than one. A bunch of crosses has less visual impact than one dominant one. A single dramatic floral arrangement makes a greater statement than a few little ones. Strive to avoid duplication of primary symbols, and a clutter of secondary symbols, as you seek to make central things central.

Worshipers and worship spaces operate in the world of symbol. With the exception of some very necessary safety or hospitality concerns, such as exit signs and restroom signs, be alert to moving out of the world of sign and into the world of symbol when developing worship space.

A symbolic vocabulary

The visual arts and forms of media embody and support the proclamation of the word of God. Principle S-16

There is great need in this postmodern, visual, and unchurched age to teach the church's symbolic vocabulary to its members and inquirers. (Some refer to this as a post-Christian era!) This generation more than many in recent history is facile in using symbols for communication. Our computers are covered with icons—a very churchy-sounding word for the technology industry. Learning to think symbolically and read the church's vocabulary of symbols are skills worthy of time and resources in Christian formation programs.

Related to this point is the ongoing question of visitor access to our worship—in other words, seeker hospitality. Without debate, we desire to be welcoming and hospitable as a church, inviting all people into our places of encounter with a loving God. The question is what this desire means and how to go about it. Some people argue that worship should be immediately understandable and accessible to the first-time visitor and that they should be invited and expected to participate immediately. Others feel that it is more hospitable to welcome visitors and seekers to worship and expect no more from them than that they observe our symbols and rites. Their participation is welcome as soon as they feel comfortable. Both models are operating in our diverse congregations.

If we agree that worship practice involves symbolic aspects, we have to agree that it takes an entire lifetime to plumb the depth of meaning of our Christian symbols, including our rites and sacraments. Whatever the model, seekers, inquirers, and new Christians should be given time to explore this symbolic world that many "cradle Christians" may take for granted. In fact many cradle Christians still desire ongoing discussion and reflection about symbols. After all, the meanings of symbols deepen as our life experience changes. Lifelong and new Christians might benefit by holding this discussion together. (To think more about this type of discussion, consider using the *Welcome to Christ* family of resources published by Augsburg Fortress.)

We have been shaped to a great degree by the Enlightenment impulse to figure out things rationally and scientifically, to describe objects and actions in an orderly, linear, and logical way. Symbols, however, are not especially orderly, linear, or logical. They can be interpreted in different ways. Their meanings can change with life experience and situation.

For reflection and discussion

1. Is the church primarily a building, primarily people, or both for you? Why?
2. How do you react to the statement that the gathered assembly (the people) is the primary symbol of Jesus in the room? Have you thought of the people in worship this way before?
3. In your worship setting are the people gathered for worship actors or audience? How does the physical worship space (architecture, furnishings, room arrangement) contribute to that perception or identity?
4. Discuss the cross in your community. How does it serve? How many crosses are there in your worship space? Do any of them move with the people, for example, in gospel processions or at the end of the service?
5. Identify recent efforts or potential opportunities to teach the symbolic vocabulary of the church to members of your community.
6. Can you think of a time when a symbol that was especially meaningful for you was offensive to another, or vice versa?

3
Encountering God Through the Ages: A Brief History

Synagogue

The earliest followers of Jesus were Jewish and worshiped with other Jews in synagogues where they gathered weekly to hear again the stories of God's call and deliverance of their forebears. We can get a flavor of those gatherings from the gospel stories where Jesus himself read from Isaiah or told the story of the Good Samaritan as an illustration of a reading from the Law and the Prophets. After the resurrection, Jesus' followers continued to go to synagogue and they also gathered, usually in someone's home, on Sunday, the day of resurrection to celebrate, remember, and expect Jesus in the way he had instructed them, by sharing a meal.

Homes, basilicas, and martyrs

Over time, the followers of Jesus did not feel welcome in the synagogues and so moved their celebration of the word to their celebration of the meal at their Sunday gathering in someone's home. Communities grew. Larger homes were needed. Some were purchased or donated and renovated to serve their new purpose, with a large room for word and meal, and another room for baptisms. The community stored offerings and conducted social ministries from there. With their exterior walls and courtyards, they were virtually indistinguishable from other homes. Other communities gathered for word and meal at the graves of a disciple or martyr or other faithful leader. Sometimes these homes or gatherings were secret for fear of persecution.

In A.D. 313, the Roman emperor Constantine legalized Christianity and made it the religion of the empire. House churches could no longer meet the needs of growing assemblies, especially in urban areas. Buildings needed to be more public. The new building of choice in the West was the Roman basilica, a rectangular general-use civic building, with a half-circle apse on one short end and the entrance on the other end, often with a courtyard leading to the entrance. These buildings usually had long rows of columns down the center that held up a central raised roof section with a high row of windows called a clerestory. Large, open spaces with plenty of light, basilicas were the all-purpose building of their day, with nothing especially religious about them. Used for legal proceedings, occasional gatherings, and warehouses, they worked well as rented buildings for worshiping communities of Christians. The establishment of Christianity allowed basilicas to be purchased or even built by congregations. The ability to own property is an important development. With ownership, the interior of a house or a basilica could be more freely arranged or modified. A long tradition of arranging platforms, furniture, and art for Christian worship began to develop.

Some communities, who had developed a tradition of worshiping at the graves of their saints and martyrs, at the grave of a disciple, or near a site important in the life of Jesus, chose to build their buildings over or near these sites.

Western developments

In time, the Church split: East and West. The Western church developed two distinct patterns of organizing itself: around bishops and around monasteries. As Europe descended into the dark ages the monasteries held much of Western civilization, including ecclesiastical art and practice, in trust. Through the Middle Ages most worship leadership roles became the sole province of educated professionals, and the assembly became primarily observers of their activity. The people rarely received communion, with the focus shifting to devotional meditation upon the sacrament. The celebration of word and meal accumulated many layers of meaning. People lost the ability to understand the Latin language of the professionals. The sacraments were mysterious and magical. Holy Communion came to be understood primarily as sacrifice. Buildings came to reflect these practices. Large areas for the professionals were created near the altar (the choir), fences and screens separated the altar and choir from the rest of the building, where people came and went, praying their own devotions, while the liturgy of the professionals continued behind the screens. Two major zones of sacred activity emerged: a place for the professionals, and a place for the laity. Occasionally a bell would ring summoning those in the main body of the church building (the nave) to pay attention, or a preacher would come out to the pulpit in this area and preach. Commerce, conversation, private devotion all might happen in the nave as the congregation milled around. (Pew seating was not introduced until the fourteenth century.)

As allegorical interpretations of worship grew, the building itself came to have special meanings. Often Gothic buildings were built in the shape of the cross to represent the body of the crucified Lord. Sometimes the chancel was even built at a little angle to the rest of the building to provide a greater allusion to the dead Lord's head. Windows told the stories of creation and redemption. Linens and vestments had functional use with allegorical meanings: the tablecloth became the burial shroud (fair linen), a small cloth to further catch spilled bread and wine became the cloth that covered Jesus face in the tomb (the corporal).

The church's first buildings were literally houses of the church (*domus ecclesiae*), a house in which the church gathered to celebrate word, bath, and meal, and from which they were sent for mission and service. By the time of the Renaissance, the buildings had become fully houses of God (*domus dei*), in which God dwelled as consecrated Holy Communion to be meditated upon devotionally; in which, like a temple, sacrifice was offered to God; into which the assembly entered perhaps with some fear and trembling; and with some areas into which only a priestly class could venture.

Reforms and reaction

The Protestant Reformation challenged many of these practices and allegorical meanings. The reformers shared a common goal of returning the people's focus to gathering around the word. Luther was also concerned with returning participation in the weekly celebration of Holy Communion to the people. Architecturally and aesthetically, reformers disagreed about how the arts serve or distract from worship. Luther was conservative in this reform, valuing the arts as tools for worship and proclamation. Other reformers went further and gutted former Catholic buildings for their own use or built very simple, plain buildings. This difference in the use of the arts can still be seen between various Protestant denominations today. The Catholic response to Protestant simplification was to further ornament church buildings and liturgies resulting in the baroque and rococo styles of church architecture. Richard Giles sums up the result as "the building, not of houses for the people of God, but of throne rooms for the shriveled fruits of division and separation, i.e., shrines for either the Host or the Book" (*Re-Pitching the Tent*, p. 43).

Participation

In the Protestant Reformation, reformed churches attempted to modify existing church buildings or develop new arrangements that architecturally served their understanding of the primacy of the word of God. Preaching in the language of the people demanded a space in which all could hear, a place for the preacher near the assembly. Participation in the weekly celebration of Holy Communion demanded that the assembly could hear, see, and draw near to the table of the Lord. Public baptisms meant the place of the bath needed to be where all could hear, see, and participate. Distinctions between clergy and laity were minimized or eliminated, and unified, multi-purpose, flexible rooms were proposed for Christian worship. This twentieth-century trend toward simplification is summarized in Louis Sullivan's famous architectural phrase, "form follows function." The church made its own version: "form follows function follows faith" (*Where We Worship*, p. 6). From this development came the concept of *centers of liturgical action*, a concept that we will examine in Chapter 4.

In some Protestant communities, hearing the word became the central focus to the exclusion of everything else. Auditoriums, lecture halls, and TV studios have been built for Christian worship. They serve one function: the audibility of the preacher. Sacraments are diminished. Art is unimportant. Assembly interaction is lost. And the community again is reduced to observing a religious professional (or a talk show host). The pendulum has swung in the other direction.

In the last 40 years Roman Catholic thought on worship environment entered a new phase as exemplified by this principle from the Constitution on the Sacred Liturgy: "The Church earnestly desires that all the faithful be led to that full, conscious, and active participation in liturgical celebrations which is called for by the very nature of the liturgy. Such participation by the Christian people as 'a chosen race, a royal priesthood, a holy nation, God's own people' (1 Peter 2:9;

see 2:4-5) is their right and duty by reason of their baptism" (Constitution on the Sacred Liturgy, Second Vatican Council, 1963). Zeal for reform led to guitar masses and some starkly gutted church buildings in the 1970s and 1980s. Having found the extremes of clerical exclusionism and anything-goes populism, Protestants and Roman Catholics alike are searching for that middle ground today.

House, temple, theatre, warehouse, courtroom, auditorium, TV studio, or lecture hall? River, baptistery, or pool? Dining room or catacomb? House of God or house of the church? In its 2000-year history the church has tried on many buildings and is ever seeking a more comfortable skin. Exactly what that skin will look like is guided by how the church understands itself, by how it worships, and by what it understands its mission to be.

For reflection and discussion

1. Describe the church buildings in which you've worshiped in your life of faith. Do they represent different historical developments of church buildings? Different understandings of worship space?
2. What's your favorite "old" church building? What's your favorite "new" church building? Why?
3. What most surprised you from this short survey of church history? What do you still wonder about?
4. What do you think all church buildings share in common?
5. What does your building say about the people who worship there?
6. How does your building shape the self-perception of the congregation that gathers in it?

4
Places of Encounter: Centers of Liturgical Action

Ecumenical consensus is emerging about what we call the spaces within our church buildings where important worship events happen: centers of liturgical action or liturgical centers. *Center* is a good word because it does not necessarily define a specific place, like a chancel, baptistery, nave, or narthex, but rather a focus that can hold meaning whether or not a specific rite is being celebrated there. It is important to remember that centers of liturgical action are more than simply furniture. These centers may move. These centers are places of activity, places where we encounter God.

Principles for Worship identifies centers of liturgical action for the ELCA:

The assembly space includes primary centers for the celebration of the word of God and the sacraments, secondary areas that facilitate the roles of all the leaders, and other spaces that complement the requirements of communal worship. Principle S-7

From this principle we infer four primary centers of liturgical action:

Place of the Assembly (body of Christ)	people	flexible space, incomplete without people
Place of the Bath (baptism)	water	font
Place of the Word (proclamation)	book	ambo
Place of the Meal (communion)	bread and wine	altar-table

The lists of centers of liturgical action vary by denomination when we compare environment and art statements. More centers may be added to the list, but usually a single place of the word, a place for the meal, and a place for the bath are included as a common core because most denominations that create these lists hold baptism and eucharist as sacraments and hold the word in high regard. Roman Catholics, who have a sacramental understanding of ministry, add the area around the priest celebrant's chair to the list to identify the priest as a symbol of Christ. Some lists include the place of daily prayer, others the place of music making, as those activities nearest word and sacrament for their communities.

Place of the assembly

We meet God in the assembly, in the warmth of a worshiper's greeting of peace, in the promise of absolution, in a song sung as we breathe as one body. God is found in the charity and love and comfort of the neighbor. The assembly *is* the body of Christ, the primary symbol of Christ in the room. As body of Christ it is bridegroom to the world. As church it is bride to Christ. Don't neglect to adorn the bride for the wedding banquet! The older categories of chancel (the front of the church) and nave (where the assembly sits) are stuck in our heads. We remember to adorn the chancel but neglect the assembly. And this center can move. The entire assembly may move from encounter to encounter. Alternatively, activity may be moved into the midst of the assembly. Move the place of the word into the midst of the people. Carve out the place of the bath from the midst of the people. Arrange the assembly so they are literally gathered around the table.

Most of the new spaces being built today could be described as unified spaces. These spaces have a single level of sacredness, made that way not by the presence of the pastor, nor by reserved bread and wine, nor because of an "eternal light." Rather, their sacred nature stems from the presence of the people of God. The place looks, should look, and is incomplete without the people.

Work to minimize the perception of stage and audience or the perception that different parts of the room are more sacred than others. Don't create a Holy of Holies. Include the assembly's place when adding temporary, seasonal art and environments. Eliminate as many artificial divides as possible: unnecessary changes in level, fences, screens, and rails. We began this process in the Reformation, and we're still working on it! Break up the illusion of assembly out there and word, meal, and bath up here. Avoid paint or color schemes or floor and wall treatments that separate the room into two parts: the place of the assembly from a place of word, meal, and bath. Individual centers of encounter may have unique floor or wall treatments, but only as they define a space in relation to the assembly.

Imagine an assembly space with a linoleum floor and painted cinderblock walls adjacent to a red carpeted platform with a pulpit, lectern, font and an altar or two all behind a fence, this area more elaborately adorned with red brick walls or wainscoting. This model is not ideal. It creates a stage and a room of observers, not participants in a communal event. It suggests that what happens on the platform makes it a more holy place, and the difference in quality of materials suggest the platform participants are more valuable than the assembly participants.

Seek to create a unified space, in which places of encounter are distinct but not separate. Perhaps the platform with the red carpet could define a single place of the word. A stone floor with a rough (nonslip) finish and a skylight might define the place of the bath. Hardwood flooring might define the place of the meal. All these are islands or oases within the linoleum-covered place of the assembly.

When preparing seasonal environments for worship we need to do more than add a few pew-end candlesticks to adorn the place of the assembly. Because of a tendency toward entertainment and stage/theatrical models, most plans usually end up with all the elaborations "in the front." This arrangement does not respect the assembly. The situation gets even worse when the stuff in the chancel is also in the way of the liturgy. I have a friend who tells stories about elaborately circuitous routes around poinsettias required of the communion ministers on Christmas Eve to accommodate the worship environment planners! Is all the liturgical action planned for the season anticipated by the environment committee? How do worship and rite planners advise the environment planners of the spatial needs of the rites?

Place of the bath

Don't you love those flume rides, with the little sign at the end of a long, hot wait that says "You will get wet on this ride"?

We meet God in the bath, in the water and the word. Water is needed for this encounter, flowing water. Water is the primary symbol in this center. Have you ever been to Shedd Aquarium in Chicago? They have whales there in a tank that faces Lake Michigan. Between the tank and the lake are a big glass wall, some sidewalks, lawn, and the lakeshore beach. But the sightlines are designed in such a way that all that stuff drops below the visitor's view. From the perspective of the viewer, the whale tank appears to be a part of the lake. Imagine if we were lucky enough to have lakeshore property for our church building (and we wanted to do baptisms year round, so needed more than that lake for a place of encounter), the kind of font that could be modeled on the Shedd Aquarium whale tank!

The place and practices of baptism proclaim the church's faith.
A generous space around flowing water reinforces the meaning of
baptism for the assembly. Principle S-8

It is surely true that "a little dab'll do ya," and that's the principle we rely upon in an emergency. But to fully grasp the power of this encounter, abundant water is preferable: deep enough to drown in, plentiful enough to bathe us clean, abundant enough to quench our thirst, flowing enough to nourish the tree of life. It is the one liturgical center that might be best permanently installed, not only because waterworks are hard to move, but also because God's work is unmoving in fidelity to our baptismal covenants. As such, if baptism can't go to the assembly, the assembly will need to go to baptism, which means the assembly will need to gather around it, or at least be able to see what happens there. They will want to participate in this encounter. Don't you see them craning their necks at every baptism in your congregation? Aren't baptismal rites often the times when the assembly seems most alive?

Minimally, at the place of the bath space must be provided to accommodate the baptismal party and include the assembly in some real way. A vessel of water is required: a font. The place of the bath needs to be waterproof and water friendly. A nonslip floor, nearby rooms for drying and changing, a paschal candle, an oasis of plants (that don't get in the way), tables for oil and candles, garments, and certificates all serve this place of encounter. Proper lighting can further define this center, together with art reflecting baptismal themes. If this liturgical center is permanently installed, special care must be given to where it is located: certainly within easy access of the assembly, but then what? To their right or left, at the entrance behind them? In the gathering space? In their midst? Placing the baptismal font near the entrance of the worship space is a powerful witness to this sacrament as our entrance into the community and gives us encouragement to return to the font regularly. We will return there many times after our baptism: for confirmation, for reconciliation, for affirmation of baptism, as new members, upon taking on new ministries, for funerals and Easter Vigils, for an entire Lenten midweek worship series perhaps, and maybe even each week, to encounter again the water of life.

At my mother's funeral, we first took her to the font. It seemed good to do. She and our father had brought each of us to the font. We had asked that the font (filled with water) be placed at the back of the worship space, one of several places it often is in this flexible room. Seating and aisles were arranged to accommodate the family and procession. The first stop in the procession was the font. There my siblings and I dressed our mother in her baptismal garment as she had dressed us in ours, covering her coffin ourselves with the white funeral pall. We remembered there Jesus' baptismal promises for her and all those who die in him. Then we continued the procession singing a baptismal hymn.

I am grateful that this worship space was flexible enough that it could accommodate our mother's coffin coming to the font. Imagine the many other times we might want to gather at the font given generous space, a strong symbol in abundant water, and an environment that suggests the fullness of the promises. We will certainly encounter rich diversity in our practice here as we work out what is right for each of our communities.

Large, abundant, permanent vessels for water are usually made of stone or ceramics. Granite is among the best materials because it is not a porous stone. Abundant stone fonts can be considered in many shapes, both historical and allegorical: six-sided, eight-sided, four-sided, round, oval, cruciform; washing tub, tomb shaped, womb shaped. Each shape suggests different baptismal images and emphases. Building a large font with flowing water is a major and exciting undertaking for a congregation. Entire books have been published about the process of preparing a congregation and a building for a font with the features described in *Principles for Worship* (see, for example, Regina Kuehn's *A Place for Baptism*, 1992).

Short of having this large permanent vessel of flowing water, interim steps can be taken. First, fill the font that you have. The water is the symbol. Put it where people can see it, touch it. And, hide the lid! Take it off. Put it away. Get rid of it. Then, begin using more water in rites. Preach and teach about the abundance of holy baptism, using all the images for baptism: washing tub, womb, tomb, watering hole, oasis, river. Go to the font more often. Take field trips to both Roman Catholic and Baptist worship spaces with generous fonts. Experiment with creating a baptismal center of encounter with a temporary large vessel of water, during Lent for example.

Place of the word

"Sir [or Madame], we would see Jesus" (John 12:21) is a classic Bible verse to carve inside of pulpits to remind preachers of their task, of what the people of God are there for: to meet the Lord, to encounter Jesus.

We meet God in the word proclaimed in our midst. The reader embodies the word as the Scriptures are proclaimed. The cantor, choir, and assembly embody the word as the psalm is sung. The preacher cracks open the word in the sermon, or more accurately, cracks us open to hear the word for our time. The primary symbol of this life-giving word is the book, the assembly's Bible or lectionary, large enough to be seen by all. The furniture on which it sits is a secondary symbol.

Placing a Bible or lectionary on an ambo or pulpit brings to visible expression the presence and importance of the word of God. Principle S-9

These activities are all proclamation of the word of God. We make no distinction between a layperson or a pastor embodying the word, and thus a single place of the word is desirable. Pulpit and lectern are replaced by an older word, *ambo*, meaning a platform, reading desk, or podium (should we choose to use one). Laity and clergy embody the word of God, each according to their gifts and callings. This single center of encounter may be defined by a platform, by an ambo, by a unique floor treatment, by lighting, by the presence of candles or floor torches or a brazier of incense to honor the word, by plants, textiles, and seasonal elaborations. These elaborations seek to bring honor to the word and the place of its proclamation. This center of action may even move seasonally, into the midst of the assembly for Christmas, Epiphany, or Easter, for example. But wherever it is, it is from there that all the ministers of the word do their proclaiming.

An ambo is best constructed of beautiful and natural materials to a human scale. It is the human who stands with the book who is embodying the word for us in worship. The ambo has a simple dignity that does not obscure the book or the minister of the word.

The most innovative ambo I've seen recently is in the Cathedral of Our Lady of the Angels in the Roman Catholic Archdiocese of Los Angeles (see it at www.olacathedral.org). The reading desk portion of the ambo is cantilevered out from its base so that virtually all of the body of the reader/preacher can be seen. It is further adjustable to accommodate readers of every height (including children) and is fully accessible to readers with limited mobility.

Avoid an ambo that suggests it is the home of the emcee, maître d', talk show host, or entertainer. Some communities prefer an ambo designed to be not only a reading desk, but to also cradle the book in a way that it can be seen and honored by the assembly. The place of the word should be well lit for reader and assembly and have a clear line of sight to the entire assembly. It should be located in a place where the reader is easily heard if acoustics are variable in the worship space.

The place of the word is probably the most flexible of the liturgical centers, and innovative communities find ways to make it speak. Explore ways that the community's Bible or lectionary can be honored here in this place of the book. How does the place of the word serve for readings arranged for multiple voices? What about proclamation accompanied by audio or visual examples? The processional cross might take up station over the shoulder of the preacher for the liturgy of the word, reminding us all that it is Christ who is the true preacher, our word of life. The place of the word may take up a temporary place in the aisle, in the midst of the assembly, surrounded by torch bearers, or a canopy of banners.

We often speak of the assembly as the body of Christ. But why don't Lutherans speak more often of the assembly as the *word* of Christ, as *becoming* the word of the Lord, embodying it as we proclaim it, carrying it in our bodies in action and witness to the world? Do we speak of the church as the word at work in the world? We speak of the Bible, and the sermon, and the power of the Spirit that way. But if we are the body of Christ in the sacramental sense, then are we not also the word of the Lord if word and sacrament are to be in balance? How can our place of the word be designed to further shape the assembly and move them to action in embodying the word?

Consider seasonal variations for this place of encounter. For example, at an Easter Vigil, we once borrowed wall art from the congregation and from around the building, one work for each of the texts we were using. Each work of art was placed on an easel near the place of the word during the reading of the text. This small collection of art then was used to adorn our worship space for the season of Easter, surrounding us with visual reminders of God's saving activity and keeping our Easter celebration before us for the fifty days leading to Pentecost. It was a great way of involving the assembly in shaping the worship environment.

Speaking of the rest of the building, here is an opportunity to connect other parts of the building with the place of the word in your worship space. Haven't you ever wondered why we aren't more creative in naming or adorning our classrooms? A series of favorite biblical stories might be a great theme for a series of rooms. Name them for favorite biblical characters or for the saints and martyrs that are meaningful for your congregation. The conference rooms in the ELCA's churchwide offices have been named for the seasons of the year. Perhaps each room might have a piece of wall art or a mural to illustrate its namesake. That artwork could come to adorn the place of the word in the worship space when its story appears in the lectionary.

Place of the meal

> Since you are the body of Christ and his members, it is your mystery that is placed on the Lord's table, it is your mystery that you receive. . . . Be what you see, and receive what you are.
> —Patrologia Latina: Augustine, Sermons 227 (PL38:1009) and 272 (PL38:1247), from *The Church for Common Prayer: A Statement on Worship Space for the Episcopal Church,* 1994.

We eat first with our eyes! Think about Thanksgiving dinner, or Easter dinner, or Christmas dinner. Why do we go to all the effort of setting a beautiful table, of arranging food on our most beautiful plates and bowls, of garnishing the dishes. We eat first with our eyes!

In *The House at Pooh Corner* Christopher Robin asks: "'What do you like doing best in the world, Pooh?' 'Well,' said Pooh, 'what I like best—' and then he had to stop and think. Because although Eating Honey *was* a very good thing to do, there was a moment just before you began to eat it which was better than when you were, but he didn't know what it was called" (A. A. Milne, pp. 306–307). A good presiding minister, a good assisting minister, a good altar guild sets us up for a "salivatory" (as in "mouth-watering") moment as they prepare the assembly and the assembly's gifts for the great thanksgiving. Sweet anticipation. We eagerly anticipate the good things to come. "Taste and see that the Lord is good!" It is Holy Communion, Lord's supper, last supper, the Supper, holy supper, eucharist, great thanksgiving, meal, wedding banquet, feast of victory, foretaste of the feast to come, Mass. Sweet anticipation. Sweet anticipation of a sweet encounter.

The table of our Lord Jesus Christ is set in the midst of the assembly. Principle S-10

Week after week we meet God in the meal, in the bread and wine and word. Bread and wine are the primary symbols. The furniture is the secondary symbol. That furniture is described as an altar-table in *Principles for Worship*. That hyphenated word seeks to get at the many dimensions of Holy Communion. It is where our Lord offers himself to us, for forgiveness of sin and for our salvation, to make us one with him. It is where he seeks us out. But it is also here around the altar-table that we share in the meal, the Lord's supper. It is in this place where the body of Christ appears, re-membered each week, as the gathered assembly, and as bread and wine. In all these ways we are in communion with God and with one another.

The ecumenical use of "table" language in principles describing the place of the eucharist suggests a desire to maintain or recover meal imagery for this sacrament. The Lord's supper was instituted at a meal, the last supper. Most of the altar-tables being built today are in a table style, rather than the tomb style of the medieval period. The furniture style shapes our perception of the event: toward family meal or toward somber sacrifice. The medieval period also gave us altar rails and all sorts of other altar and chancel appointments that today compete with the bread and wine for importance and with our understanding of Holy Communion as meal.

Like the ambo, the altar-table should be constructed of beautiful and natural materials to a human scale, well-lit, and with a simple dignity. The standardized height for an altar-table is 39–40 inches tall, scaled to accommodate a presiding minister. Other dimensions should be scaled to the size of the worship space.

As a meal of the assembly, we need to be able to gather around the altar-table. Greater value is being placed on developing altar-tables that the assembly can gather around. That means at least that the presiding minister, serving in the place and stead of Christ (*The Book of Concord*, p. 178), should be able to face the congregation across the altar-table. If we can do more than that, we seek to eliminate barriers between the assembly and the altar-table. Extra steps that we once valued as signs of God's transcendence—going up to a high place to pray—now seem to impede people as we invite them to come and see Jesus (taste and see that the Lord is good), and experience God's immanence, God's closeness. Our concerns for hospitality lead us toward spaces with fewer steps, with ramps that allow everyone access. To gather around the altar-table also means we'll need generous space around it that graciously receives the assembly and allows them to come and go, and facilitates the work of their communion ministers. As usual, candles or floor torches, plants, and lighting can serve to further define and adorn this place of encounter.

Vessels are necessary for serving. Some communities value precious metal tableware, the best they can afford, to hold this life-giving food. Other communities value glass or crystal so the primary symbols of bread and wine are not obscured. Others value stoneware or pottery in keeping with the simplicity of this meal. No matter the material, we value well-designed and well-crafted vessels and textiles that honor the body of Christ. The primary cup and plate should be large enough to be seen by the entire assembly. Beyond the bread and cup, anything else placed on the altar-table is distracting and competes with these primary symbols.

Many of our buildings are absolutely symmetrical, with the altar-table anchoring the centerline. Symmetry is a very strong architectural feature. This placement of the altar-table we also inherited from medieval theology and architecture. The altar was the central thing. But what if we want the assembly to be the central thing? Or word and sacrament to be in balance? Historically, eastern churches have done a better job with that, using a more circular or square plan for their buildings. But we need to work with what we have. *Principles for Worship* suggests that the community's altar-table need not be spatially centered (application S-10D, p. 80). It shares focus with other places of encounter, with the other centers of liturgical action. This begs the question, which will be answered differently in every context, "How will the centers of liturgical action interact with one another and with the assembly in our worship space?"

Flexibility of space and portability of furniture facilitate the variations of worship as well as related activities of congregation and community. Principle S-19

Other spaces

The worship space includes designated spaces for worship leaders. The place for presiding and assisting ministers is distinct, but not overly separated or elevated. Principle S-11

Though not a center of liturgical action in the strict sense, our worship spaces must also provide for a place for worship leaders, including the presiding minister, assisting minister and other lay worship ministers, and the cantor, musicians, and choir. As we have seen, for some denominations the chair or place of the presiding minister is a formal and distinct center of liturgical action, but Lutherans understand all the worship leaders, musicians included, as part of the assembly. And the kind of environment they need to serve effectively is functionally only a little different from what the rest of the assembly needs. The presiding minister and other lay worship leaders need a place from which to lead the assembly where they can be seen by all. That might mean a platform to enhance their visibility, or at least clear sightlines to the entire assembly. Also useful are well-designed chairs to accommodate vestments and support good posture and vocalization, good lighting, good acoustics perhaps with sound system access, generous space allowing for leadership from their chairs, nearby tables for worship supplies, and easy access to the place of the bath, word, and meal.

Providing adequate areas for choirs and instrumentalists allow them to function effectively as worship leaders. Principle S-12

Musicians are also integral worship ministers whose primary responsibility is to lead the assembly's song. As such, they are part of the assembly. Musicians need space for gathering and for instruments from which they can lead effectively. Good chairs for posture and vocal support, good lighting, good acoustics, flexible and generous space, easy access to the font, ambo, altar-table, and nearby storage are marks of a serving environment for musicians. For all worship leaders, easy access to rehearsal spaces and preparation spaces (sacristies) and the gathering place, is also ideal. My own preference for a sacristy is adjacent to the gathering space and the assembly's entrance to the worship space, facilitating interaction between the ministers and the gathering assembly before the liturgy and more easily accommodating preparation for processions. This location may better serve baptismal, funeral, and wedding parties as well.

Processional and gathering spaces are also important to include in any plan. Without generous processional space surrounding the centers of liturgical action the assembly is locked into their pews or chairs. Liturgy and sacraments and seasonal rites are activities, events. They involve movement by leaders and by the assembly. Think carefully about how to provide for all the movement of the rites that we celebrate throughout the year. Beware of obstructing the processional space during seasonal or occasional worship activities.

Finally, the centers of liturgical action don't stand alone. Effective buildings gather and send. They invite the assembly into these places of encounter. Hospitable signs guide people from the street or parking area to the main ritual entrance, usually the one most convenient to the worship space. Ideally, the building's ritual entrance (the one used for funerals and weddings) *invites* into gathering or hospitality space, which further invites to the font, to the place of the assembly, and to the word, and the meal. Effectively arranged spaces also *send* to mission and ministry in the world, to fellowship, and to faith formation.

I once visited a worship space where the gathering space provided this incredible sense of hospitality and sensitivity to the transition from the liturgy to the world. Great care had been taken in its design. The room was filled with light and minimally furnished around its perimeter. Large beautiful doors at each end of the room opened up to the world and the place of worship in a creative tension. From each set of doors a few steps (and a ramp) descended into the gathering space. In the center of this generous space was a beautiful long oak table. It was here where guests and worshipers were offered welcome, hospitality, and refreshment before or after worship. This table was crafted well enough that it could have easily served as the community's altar-table. But it was not. The altar-table was visible through the doors (and across the font) in the worship space. It was equally well crafted. They were a ministry team. Something about that oak table has lived with me. Its intentionality about gracious hospitality. Its wonderful tension with the altar-table. Its centrality. Its eager welcome. Its promise of more to come. Its permanence. Its language of meal rather than transaction. Since then I've longed for that beautiful oak table every time I've been at a church reception with a beat-up 8-foot folding table holding up an electric coffee urn.

For reflection and discussion

1. Are the centers of liturgical action described in this chapter—the place of the assembly, word, bath, and meal—well defined in your worship space? How do they relate to the assembly?

2. Where is your congregation's baptismal font located? What is striking about it? What might its location or physical features reveal about your congregation's understanding of baptism? What might these things communicate to a visitor?

3. How is your place of the meal related to your frequency of celebration of the meal?

4. Does your congregation have one or two (or more) places from which the word is proclaimed? (Consider both the public reading of scripture and preaching.) What conclusions do you draw from that practice?

5. We often hear the assembly referred to as the body of Christ. Talk about what it would mean if we spoke more often of the assembly as the embodied word of God.

6. How balanced is your preparation of all four liturgical centers when creating seasonal worship environments? Consider particularly Advent/Christmas or Lent/Easter.

5
Sacred Space:
What Makes Space Sacred?

Why is space sacred?

We've looked at different kinds of church buildings through history. We've examined the places where Israel worshiped. We've imagined our own worship spaces and remembered ones from our past. Many of these spaces have achieved the status of "sacred space." It's time to examine what exactly we mean when we say something is *sacred*.

We begin with our theology of creation and of the incarnation and of the church or assembly. God blessed of all the created order, named it good, and further blessed it by becoming one with it through the Incarnation. Our ideas of what makes a space holy will follow from God's actions in making the world holy.

God's creation makes space sacred

Genesis 1 reveals God's evaluation of the work of creation: "God saw everything that he had made, and indeed, it was very good" (Gen. 1:31a). We take seriously God's Genesis proclamation of a creation that is good in God's sight. In that sense God makes all spaces sacred. Here we find the sacredness of natural beauty.

The discipline of environment and art for worship is all about created matter and space being used in ways that honor and adore the Trinity and that make Christ known. We seek to make space for an encounter. Space that honors the Trinity honors creation, and space that honors creation is space that is genuine and authentic, not synthetic or pretending to be something that it is not. It is made of materials that are God-grown, from the abundance of creation, respectfully used, and that are beautiful and well crafted. It is space that has changing interest over the course of the day or season. It is space that respects the earth and is at home in its natural environment. It is space that contains multivalent symbols (remember Chapter 2) that speak through all the changes and chances of life. In sacred spaces, beauty and justice can walk hand in hand. This sacred goodness means, for example, that we avoid using materials that pretend to be something they are not, thereby denying the realities of the creation. Living plants or flowers harvested from people's gardens, then, are preferable to silk flowers; fine furniture made from natural materials is preferable to wood-grain plastic laminate; real wax candles are preferable to electric or tube candles.

In the worship space, beauty is a portal to the mystery of God and a witness to Christian faith and truth. Beauty is revealed through the honest use of the materials of God's creation. Principle S-20

God's incarnation makes space sacred

The incarnation further sanctifies the whole creation as sacred space. The incarnation is the presence of God among us in Jesus Christ. "The Word became flesh and dwelt among us," says John's gospel (John 1:14a). That the Lord of the universe took on the flesh of creation, lived, walked, ate, died, and was raised makes creation sacred. And God remains graciously present to us today. Jesus' resurrection let loose the power of his Spirit upon the creation. Jesus promised to remain with us, in his followers, the body of Christ, in word, meal, and bath. Sacred spaces can make Christ present. Sacred spaces can be incarnational.

Basic requirements for humans when they gather, together with what we know of how Jesus used space, set the norms for our worship spaces. Jesus used vessels, texts, and created matter in his worship and ministry. Space that honors the incarnation is space that invites a relationship, embodies the Lord, builds up the body of Christ, transforms, introduces Christ. And for Christians, this presence of Christ makes a space holy:

- Christ present in the living Word—in the assembly, in the sacraments of meal and bath, in the proclamation of biblical readings and the sermon
- Christ present in incarnational arts (art that makes Christ present)
- Christ present in creation as it is used in sacraments, buildings, furnishings, art, musical instruments, and seasonal environments

So what does it mean to strive for use of art and environment that makes Christ present? In the gospel for the Second Sunday of Easter, Thomas needed something (someone) to see in order to believe. He needed to touch. Seeing is believing. Touching is believing. In the story of the paralytic and others like it, people came to the disciples and said, "Sir, we would see Jesus." The woman in the crowd reached out and touched Jesus. Disciples still taste bread and wine to remember Jesus.

The Spirit brings faith, but Jesus knew that to grow in faith, we would need to see and touch and taste. He gave us bread and wine and water to touch and taste and see and smell and hear as symbols of his presence. In the spirit of the Word Made Flesh, Emmanuel, we seek to use incarnational arts to assist people to touch Jesus, to taste Jesus, to feel Jesus, to see Jesus, to meet Jesus. That's why we come together, of course, week after week, on the first day of the week: to meet Jesus, to hear the story again. It's our favorite story. We love to hear it. We never tire of it. We're used to meeting Jesus on the first day of the week, in the community, in the bread, wine, water, and word. When seekers, the unbaptized, the uncatechized, baptismal candidates, catechism students and the newly baptized, the bruised or weak in faith come to us and plead, "Sir/Madame, we would see Jesus," what do we do so that they may respond in faith, "It is the Lord! We have seen the Lord!"? When the assembly gathers each Sunday, what expectation do we have of our buildings or worship environments to make Christ present?

God's people make space sacred

The body of Christ gathered in prayer hallows the space used for worship. Principle S-4

Christian worship space is not sacred because of any architectural feature or any particular worship appointment. For Christians, sacredness is not determined by the presence of things but by the presence of people. Ultimately only people, not things, grow in sacredness. Our presence as the people of God, as the body of Christ, as a baptizing people makes places where we gather sacred. Christ's presence in us makes us sacred. Now we can say that holy people make a holy space. The presence of the people of God, the body of Christ, sanctifies a space more than any other activity or experience or feeling does. In fact, the most common way to dedicate a church is to use it—to celebrate communion there—for the first time. The places where we gather weekly to celebrate word and meal, the places from which we are sent out in holy mission become for us "sacred places." It is in these places where we are reminded again who we are, whose we are, and how we are to live. It is in these places where we are re-formed into a baptizing people, bringing Christ to the world.

What makes space sacred?

The question "What makes a sacred space?" cannot be left entirely to the emotions. The answer contains much more than the subjective feeling that we all have about our favorite places of retreat, deliverance, natural beauty, prayer, or meditation. Space is not value neutral. Spaces are containers for symbolic communication, and symbols form people.

Spaces, sacred or secular, form people for good or ill. They are catechetical but not didactic. That means they form us, our faith, and our understandings of God and the church, by "whispering in our ear" more than by teaching logically arranged information and content to master. How we shape our spaces is becoming more critical as we encounter more and more people with no previous experience of the gospel. Because, for them, the first whispers of the gospel they may hear may very well come from our worship spaces.

Lawrence Hoffman, in his book *Sacred Places and the Pilgrimage of Life* identifies three types of sacred places: those of natural beauty, those of historical significance, and those made holy by human ritual. Christian experience as people of God includes all three types.

Natural beauty

Natural wonders and other places of great natural beauty are inherently sacred. We can all stand in awe at the edge of the Grand Canyon, Niagara Falls, or at the seashore. Perhaps it's your favorite fishing hole, or revealed in your microphotography of the surface of a woodland creek. Maybe it's the desert or the wide-open expanse of Big Sky country, a jagged Colorado mountain range or the blue-shrouded Appalachian hills. These sacred places can be subjective, but most would agree about their basic beauty and the sense of awe they create for the creature contemplating the creator.

Historical significance
Some places become sacred over time because something significant
happened there. That was true for the Israelites, for the early church,
and is still true for us. For Israel, sacred places were first places of historical significance, places where God delivered them. In the story of
Jacob's dream,

> Jacob himself puts it beautifully. After falling asleep on what he
> thought was God-forsaken terrain, he awakens to see the ladder
> connecting heaven and earth. "Surely God is in this place," he
> concludes, "but I did not know it." Appropriately, he names the
> place: It is Beth El, "the house of God" (*Sacred Places,* p. 9).

Places where God delivered Israel were often marked with a monument, called an *ebenezer*. Often when Israel returned to those places
they remembered God's saving activity. Over the centuries Israel's
nomadic lifestyle became more settled. Then those saving acts began
to be remembered in time, on a calendar, rather than by returning to
the site of deliverance.

The church eventually developed its own calendar of God's saving
activity through Jesus Christ, though pilgrims have always traveled to
Jerusalem, Nazareth, Galilee, and Bethlehem to visit important sites
from the life of Christ.

Human ritual and artistic creation
In a similar way, God's saving activity in our own lives makes spaces
sacred over time. For my family, that space is an ELCA church building in rural eastern South Dakota near where our family from
Trondheim, Norway, settled in 1879. Both the farm (where I have
never lived) and the church (where I have never been a member) are
sacred places of a sort. These places have achieved a sacred status in the
family because they're where the weddings are held. They're where the
funerals are held. We are there for Christmas or Thanksgiving. Those

1879 immigrants and most of every generation since then are buried there. It's where we go to hear the promise of the resurrection. It's where we expect Christ to come again. It was the right place for my ordination. It was where my sisters chose to be married, on the same spot where our parents were married. Sites acquire sacredness over time, like a tree or a pearl, which year in and year out lays down new layers of growth. I've lived in Michigan, Tennessee, Ohio, Wisconsin, and now Minnesota, and it is always to these sacred places that we return to see family, to worship together, for summer pilgrimages, holiday celebrations, and rites of passage. It's where we expect to meet Christ.

When they are new, these kinds of spaces are not naturally sacred, nor has any saving event yet occurred there. They are selected for other reasons, perhaps because that's where the Division for Outreach discovered a need for a new congregation, or where a mission congregation looking to build their first building found available land at a major intersection. Maybe the land was a donated farm field for a landlocked, small-town congregation building a new accessible sanctuary. Maybe enough immigrant Trondheimers had settled west of the river that they could create a new community of faith. Most parish church buildings find themselves in this category. These sites need help in establishing their sacredness. That's why they are usually marked as sacred by some sign. A dedication rite is one such common sign. We dedicate churches, not to change them in their basic nature, but to begin to set them apart as a tool in God's saving work. Uniquely ecclesial architecture is a further sign.

Over time, as these church buildings accommodate weekly Sunday morning worship, baptisms, funerals, family events, and annual Easter and Christmas celebrations, their sense of sacred space grows. This sacred sense can be both a blessing and a curse as every person knows who has ever been involved in a process to change, renew, or replace a worship space.

These sites are sacred because the people who gather there are sacred. And over time, we become attached to those spaces because of our history with them. If the assembly's needs change and the building must change, or we outgrow the space, or we can't "get this thing to serve" without moving or rebuilding or renewing we must deal pastorally and respectfully with the range of emotions (grief, fear, excitement, hope) that the assembly will have about this sacred place, this place of encounter, this place where they have come to expect to find God.

Principles for Worship is careful not to make too great a claim for any action on our part in making a space sacred. God's activity in forming us as the body of Christ and God's presence in the word and the sacraments are what make spaces functionally sacred for us. That sense of sacredness remains attached to the people and the means of grace, more than to any specific place. "The body of Christ gathered in prayer hallows the space used for worship. The worshiping assembly is a place where God makes a home. Christ's presence is promised not under certain architectural forms but where two or three are gathered in his name" (principle S-4 and background S-4A, p. 71). In that sense, sacred spaces can be sold, abandoned, or repurposed. These actions may be pastorally and emotionally difficult because of an assembly's accumulated history, but they are not theologically difficult.

Sacred space is formational and evangelical

We can further say that sacred space is always formational and can be evangelical, two foundational stones for Lutheran thinking about worship space. The following chapters will take up those concerns. It is sufficient to say here that for any denomination, worship space is formational, for good and for ill, and worship leaders are wise to always consider how their spaces are shaping their assemblies, and conversely, how their understandings of being church shape their spaces.

Additionally, Lutherans, who define themselves as an assembly among whom the gospel is preached in its purity, should be further concerned that sacred spaces, our worship spaces, are evangelical, that is, that they proclaim the gospel in their very composition, arrangement, and materials.

Can sacred space be ordinary space?

Sacred space may at times also serve ordinary purposes. There is nothing particularly sacred about making the church building available for a concert, for a foot-care clinic for the elderly, or for the weekly Narcotics Anonymous, Suicide Survivors, or other community meetings. Many of our church buildings are used as polling places. These activities are secular (i.e. not sacred), but they are certainly not antithetical to the gospel purpose. It is our concern for mission, for justice, for being hospitable, for the abundant life of the entire community that motivates us to open the doors. It that sense, we may have a sacred motivation, but our guests' activities are ordinary, functional.

A hospitable worship space generously accommodates the assembly, its liturgy, and a broad range of activities appropriate to the life of the congregation and its surrounding community. Principle S-17

Holy mission sanctifies space

The ongoing challenge for congregations is the continuing evaluation of whether their spaces are serving them well, continually asking the question, "How are we gonna get this thing to serve?" Do all of our words make a great claim that is missing from our actions or from our buildings? Does the building stand up to the words of the liturgy? Is the building hospitably gathering, transforming through word and sacrament, and lovingly sending the assembly for the sake of the world? Are we designing the space or using the space in ways that help form congregations into evangelical, missionary, baptizing communities?

For reflection and discussion

1. What does it mean that "God makes the world holy"? Can the whole creation be holy?
2. Name some examples of how your worship space has acquired a sense of holiness for you because of the history you have praying there.
3. Name as many sites of sacred deliverance from Israel's history that you can think of and recall their stories.
4. How does your worship space make Christ present for worshipers? What gets in the way?
5. Name one or two spaces in your life that fit into each of the following categories:

   Places of natural beauty
   Places of historical significance
   Places of human ritual and artistic creation

6
Evangelical Space: Worship Space Makes Christ Known

Anyone who is to find Christ must first find the Church. For how can one know where Christ is, and where faith in him is, unless he knew where his believers are? Whoever wishes to know something about Christ must not trust to himself, nor by the help of his own reason build a bridge of his own to heaven, but must go to the Church, must visit it, and make inquiry. Now the Church is not wood and stone, but the company of people who believe in Christ; He must keep in company with them, and see how they believe, and teach, and live.
—Martin Luther, from *The Lutheran Liturgy*, 1947

Sacred space is evangelical

There are ". . . tongues in trees, books in running brooks, and sermons in stones."
—William Shakespeare, *As You Like It*

Do our worship spaces make Christ known? Do our worship spaces invite people to encounter the Christ, the one who we believe is Lord of the future, the one who has made a difference in our lives? How well do we provide space for that encounter in the word, the meal, the bath, and the assembly? Contrary to the impression given by American individualism, we are not saved on our own. We are assured of our salvation by our initiation (baptism) into Christian community, into the body of Christ. There are no free-lance Christians. Noah's ark is used as an image of the church for good reason. We are in the boat together. (And as bad as the stink sometimes is on the inside, it's better than the storm on the outside!) Do we provide an environment that introduces people to Christ through human contact, through word and sacrament, ritual action, prayer and proclamation, through incarnational arts? Are our worship environments filled with the truth about Jesus Christ?

This question may be a uniquely Lutheran way to address the issue, though certainly it is a concern of every Christian communion. But our history and heritage keep us particularly edgy about clear proclamation of the gospel. We seek to ground everything in the word. Have we thought seriously about grounding our worship spaces in the word too? We've been inoculated by our history to have, or perhaps be, antibodies in this part of the body of Christ, always seeking out those things that might get in the way of clear proclamation of the gospel. So when it comes to sacred space or worship space, we ask: how is the space telling the story, proclaiming the good news of Jesus Christ, welcoming the stranger, freeing the captive, loosing the bonds, allowing an encounter, telling the truth? "How does this thing serve?"

This encounter is shaped by more than architecture. All the arts must be considered. All the arts proclaim the gospel and our heritage is to use every available media in that proclamation, arts included. Electronic art forms are becoming a part of that encounter in more and more of our assemblies.

Marks of the worship environment

We seek to maintain worship environments that are hospitable (principle S-17), clearly defined (S-18), flexible (S-19), and beautiful (S-20). These categories are further examined in Huffman, Van Loon, and Stauffer's *Where We Worship* (pp. 28–38).

We want our spaces to be *hospitable*, to welcome not only the member and guest, but to welcome Christ—in the assembly and in word and sacrament. We want to be sure people of all kinds feel at home, regardless of gender, race, age, class, ethnic background, and ability. Who is the most gracious host or hostess you know? Seek to emulate that person's style and grace. Engage such hosts and hostesses to lead your congregation's ministry of hospitality.

Clearly defined spaces keep primary things primary, are free of nonessentials and duplicated symbols. Assembly, word, bath, and meal are the primary things. Minimize the clutter. Our church buildings, like our homes, accumulate objects over time. Honor memorial gifts in a memorial book, in open sacristy shelving or in archival display cases. Put away worship appointments that are not needed this season or are duplicated. Select appropriate appointments for each season and rotate from the collection. Some things may be simply worn out and discarded. Or they are evaluated and found not to serve well. Seek out good design, quality construction, and honest use of natural materials. Consider the best quality you desire and can afford for your home and plan accordingly for your worship space.

A *flexible* space is one that serves the assembly and the liturgical work it needs to do through the changing liturgies of the church's year and the rites of passage that are celebrated as needed. It allows the focus and emphasis to shift according to the needs of the assembly and the lectionary. It allows for seasonal variation. It allows the assembly to come and go and move as the rites suggest. It is barrier free. It invites participation.

Principle S-20 in *Principles for Worship* addresses *beauty:*

In the worship space, beauty is a portal to the mystery of God and a witness to Christian faith and truth. Beauty is revealed through the honest use of the materials of God's creation. Principle S-20

Principle S-20 goes on to quote the new Roman Catholic environment and art statement:

> Art chosen for the place of worship is not simply something pretty or well made, an addition to make the ordinary more pleasant. . . . Rather, artworks truly belong in the church when they are worthy of the place of worship and when they enhance the liturgical, devotional, and contemplative prayer they are inspired to serve (*Built of Living Stones*, p. 29).

So we see that we are not talking merely about decoration, but about art that serves the church, enhances places of encounter, and proclaims the gospel.

Arts proclaim the gospel

The Use of the Means of Grace says, "Music, the visual arts, and the environment of our worship spaces embody the proclamation of the Word in Lutheran churches. . . . The visual arts and the spaces for worship assist the congregation to participate in worship, to focus on the essentials, and to embody the Gospel" (principle 11 and application 11B).

The arts are vehicles for proclamation. Our witness with language is one form of proclamation. The sermon uses homiletical and rhetorical arts and our readers employ the art of effective oral presentation. Our hymns and musical tradition provide another major proclamatory art form for Lutherans. Other arts serve as vehicles for proclamation as well. We have not abandoned the visual arts to proclaim the gospel as some other Protestants did at the time of the Reformation.

Art and architecture proclaim the gospel, enrich the assembly's participation in the word and sacraments, and reinforce the themes of the occasion and season. Liturgical art animates the life and faith of the community. Principle S-5

Evangelical space seeks to facilitate an encounter

Decorating the mall or even our homes for the holidays is different from creating a seasonal worship environment or worship space. Creating permanent, seasonal, or occasional environments for worship is more than decorating. It is an act of faith. It is about creating an environment that fosters prayer, fosters an encounter. Arts for worship are not for ornamentation but for evocation. They are evangelical, proclamatory, revelatory, incarnational, and epiphanic. Involving the community in creating art for worship can be faith building. Effective art for worship helps people to encounter God in new ways through the images of the season or event. Effective art for worship can proclaim the kingdom of God in ways that words or music cannot, though they are complementary and overlapping.

We can look to Good Friday's adoration of the crucified for an example of the assembly creating its own evangelical art during the course of the liturgy. The presiding minister introduces a cross to the assembly with the words, "Behold the life-giving cross on which was hung the salvation of the whole world." That cross can then be placed within an environment that gives it honor: with torches, votive screens, or plants for example. The assembly then may be invited to participate in adoration of the crucified by individually moving to the cross, and placing votive candles around the symbol with prayer. The result is seasonal art for worship that is much more than decoration. It is a work created by the whole assembly: the artists in the group through their direction and planning, the presiding minister with a worthy cross, and the assembly with their candles and prayers. Contrast the meaning this temporary art may carry by the end of the encounter with the stereotypical split-rail fence cross in a Christmas-tree stand draped with a purple cloth.

Often the preparation of our worship spaces for the seasons of the church year has been left up to the altar guild. Let me suggest an alternate model. Consider separating seasonal environment preparation from weekly liturgy preparation and raising up distinct groups for each. The altar guild might be defined to function in weekly liturgy preparation. Seasonal environment groups can be gathered annually from the assembly as intergenerational groups of men and women and children charged with preparing the worship space for a given season. This model allows more people to be involved in worship ministries, allows for innovation and creativity, and turns the assembly into active participants. A budget and plan may be developed by each group and coordinated through the worship committee.

House of God (domus dei) or house of the church (domus ecclesiae)?

On my way to worship I drive past a big church building. On that building, across the lintel above the front door, is carved in huge letters: "This is the house of God and the gate of heaven,"—a vision of the *domus dei*. Found printed at the top of a Sunday service folder: "Be thoughtful, be silent, and be reverent; for this is the House of God. BEFORE the service speak to the Lord; DURING the service let the Lord speak to you; AFTER the service speak to one another." This congregation (or pastor) understands their worship space to be *domus dei*.

In the church building where I worship, the worship space is not much larger than a house. The art is all domestic scale. There is only one step between the altar-table and the assembly. The whole congregation can get into the narthex and around the font for a baptism. No sound system is needed. There is no eternal light. The simple white stucco walls, hardwood floors, and pews look empty and rather plain when no assembly is present. There is no steeple or stained glass to speak of. The building is a *domus ecclesiae*.

Every church building is a combination of *domus dei* and *domus ecclesiae*. How they are combined reveals something about the assembly that worships there. Most denominations today lean toward house of the church as they describe their worship buildings, with house of God representing an understanding of something more like a temple, shrine, monument, or dwelling place for God.

Principles for Worship leans toward an understanding of church building as *domus ecclesiae*: "The body of Christ gathered in prayer hallows the space used for worship . . . the worshiping assembly is a place where God makes a home" (principle S-4 and background S-4A, p. 71). How do you understand your place of worship: house of God, house of the people, or some of both? Does this understanding come from how you understand God is present there? What about the language your congregation uses to describe where they worship: sanctuary, centrum, worship center? How does language give clues or help to shape that understanding? When Lutherans use the word *sanctuary* it usually means the whole place of worship (chancel, nave, and narthex together). For Roman Catholics, *sanctuary* means what Lutherans call the "chancel." Are these distinctions helpful when considering a unified space with multiple centers of liturgical action that are more integrally related to the assembly? *Sanctuary* also has meanings that suggest a place of safety, a place set apart, separate from the world. Is that what we want to suggest, a place where we separate ourselves from the world for reinvigoration and refreshment in order to be strengthened for service? Perhaps. Or does it suggest an escape from the world and from our responsibility as the body of Christ active in it? Worship spaces with stained glass, no natural lighting, in fortress-like buildings, separated from the changing seasons at the end of meandering and confusing hallways are certainly effective at keeping the world out. On the other hand, they may invite an experience of the holy. Modern buildings with their superstructure exposed and clear plate-glass windows showing the traffic moving outside certainly let the world in and might be more comfortable for the stranger, but they remind others more of the workplace, the mall, and the convention center than a place of encounter with God.

House of God or house of the church? Sanctuary or worship center? Modern (or postmodern) or traditional? There is no single "Lutheran" answer. But these are important questions to ask when we're trying to figure out, "How are we gonna get this thing to serve?"

Making theological, pastoral, and aesthetic decisions

So, how shall we evaluate our spaces? Lutherans, as a group united by certain theological understandings, will make theological evaluations of space and art for worship. Pastoral judgments are also required for the local context and for the sake of the encounter. And aesthetics (quality, taste, and style) matter. Is this worthy and effective art for worship?

Principles for Worship, seeking to be descriptive of good practice, lays out Lutheran principles for creating an environment for worship in ways that local congregations can apply to their own contexts. These principles can be applied to church buildings built in any architectural style, of any size or material, of any age or budget. They can be applied to projects large or small, elements old or new. The goal is to make principle-based decisions in order that our spaces serve well.

A methodology for evaluation

Consider this methodology for evaluating worship environments and appointments, for existing spaces and for the building of new spaces.

THEOLOGICAL EVALUATION (primary)

⇓　　 if passes

PASTORAL EVALUATION (secondary)

⇓　　 if passes

AESTHETIC EVALUATION (tertiary)

⇓　　 if passes

IMPLEMENTATION

This methodology moves intentionally through three criteria. In practice its operation is more fluid than it appears in a diagram. A variation might be to ask theological, pastoral, and aesthetic questions without giving one criterion preference over another, but that seems too loose for Lutherans, whose identity is rooted in theological documents and understandings. There needs to be some prioritization of these criteria.

Here is a simple example of how a congregation might use this model. The congregation where I worship conducted a self-study with *Principles for Worship* as we considered changes to our narthex, to our musicians' space, and responded to other congregational concerns. For three weeks our task group, chartered by the congregational council, solicited feedback about these areas of concern from the congregation. Several worshipers suggested that we consider air conditioning for our worship space. How did we evaluate air conditioning using this model? First theologically: Neither the Bible nor the confessions nor *The Use of the Means of Grace* have anything to contribute about air conditioning from a theological point of view. Evaluating theologically, air conditioning is "neutral."

We proceeded to the next criterion. Pastorally, both positives and negatives could be listed. The task group considered air conditioning to be first of all an evangelism issue. To hospitably welcome people to worship, the time had come when the absence of air conditioning might be a stumbling block for people with respiratory or heart conditions, or for those who would just seek a more comfortable place to worship. On the negative side, air conditioning could be seen as a luxury or conspicuous consumption (in our region). Aesthetically (the third level of evaluation), the committee decided that air conditioning would be nice to have. Our written report concluded: "Though not a priority, the task group recommends that air conditioning be considered at a time when the furnace is in need of attention/replacement."

This example "passed" all three criteria. In other cases, a project may proceed even if it has not passed all three. For example, a preacher may want to make a theological or pastoral point in a sermon with a bad piece of art. In that case, the art in question might be kitschy, but would serve a theological and pastoral purpose. Aesthetically, we would know it is bad (and know not to keep it around in a Sunday school classroom). In some cases, the theological consideration may be important enough that both pastoral and aesthetic implications must be worked out.

For each criterion, the assembly will need to identify a standard by which it will judge. Typically that will be authoritative documents or understandings. An ELCA congregation might consider these tools or standards for evaluation:

THEOLOGICAL
The Use of the Means of Grace
Principles for Worship
Biblical and Lutheran confessional principles

PASTORAL
Principles for Worship
Pastoral principles like those outlined throughout this book
Americans with Disabilities Act resources and documents
Our experience as the people of God

AESTHETIC
Our experience as the people of God
Our experience of God's creation
The experience of trained artists and designers

Whether you are convinced by the multi-level approach or not, a group can benefit from the value in the three-criteria evaluation method. Theology, pastoral considerations, and aesthetics matter when where trying to figure out "how we're gonna get this thing to serve."

A question of taste

Aesthetics within a worship space matter because style, taste, artistry, and quality are involved in the way people find and determine meaning—meaning in songs, in art, in worship, in life. Different styles whisper in the ear in different ways. This truth is at the source of much of our differing opinions about music for worship. An aesthetic judgment must be made along with theological and pastoral judgment when evaluating what happens in and around the Christian assembly.

The first steps in making aesthetic judgments is learning to recognize and appreciate what others see. Frank Burch Brown developed this methodology for learning to see and evaluate the aesthetic dimension of the Christian life in three steps (*Good Taste, Bad Taste, & Christian Taste*, pp. xi, 13–23):

- Step 1: perceiving (apperception): "taking in the features of a particular work of art, or noticing the aesthetic qualities of a natural object" (p. 13). This step is affected by our education, experience, and cultural heritage.
- Step 2: enjoying (appreciation): learning to appreciate the work, the meaning it holds, whether you enjoy it or not.
- Step 3: judging (appraisal): how you evaluate to the extent that you will make a public claim about it.

Brown's book also does leading work examining the question of Christian taste. He makes these twelve assumptions for testing Christian taste (pp. 250–251):

1. There are many kinds of good taste, and many kinds of good religious art and music. In view of cultural diversity, it would be extremely odd if that were not true.

2. Not all kinds of good art and music are equally good for worship, let alone for every tradition or faith community. In terms of worship, therefore, it is not enough that a work or style of art be likeable; it must also be appropriate.

3. Various appropriately Christian modes can be used to mediate religious experience artistically—from radically transcendent to radically immanent in a sense of the sacred; from exuberantly abundant to starkly minimal in means; from prophetic to pastoral in tone; from instructive to meditative in aim.

4. Every era and cultural context tends to develop new forms of sacred music and art, which to begin with often seem secular to many people.

5. Because every musical/aesthetic style calls for a particular kind of attunement, no one person can possibly be competent to make equally discerning judgments about every kind of music or art. Yet almost everyone is inclined to assume or act otherwise. That impulse is related to the sin of pride.

6. It is an act of Christian love to learn to appreciate or at least respect what others value in a particular style or work that they cherish in worship or in the rest of life. That is different, however, from personally liking every form of commendable art, which is impossible and unnecessary.

7. Disagreements over taste in religious music (or any other art) can be healthy and productive; but they touch on sensitive matters and often reflect or embody religious differences as well as aesthetic ones.

8. The reasons why an aesthetic work or style is good or bad, weak or strong (and in what circumstances), can never be expressed fully in words; yet they can often be pointed out through comparative—and repeated—looking and listening.

9. Aesthetic judgments begin with, and owe special consideration to, the community or tradition to which a given style or work is indigenous or most familiar. But they seldom end there; and they cannot, if the style or work is to invite the attention of a wide range of people over a period of time.

10. The overall evaluation of any art used in worship needs to be a joint effort between clergy, congregation, and trained artists and musicians, taking into account not only the aesthetic qualities of the art itself but also the larger requirements and contours of worship, which should at once respond to and orient the particular work of art or music.

11. Although relative accessibility is imperative for most church art, the church also needs art—including "classic" art of various kinds—that continually challenges and solicits spiritual and theological growth in the aesthetic dimension. This is art that the Christian can grow into but seldom out of.

12. Almost every artistic style that has been enjoyed and valued by a particular group over a long period of time and for a wide range of purposes has religious potential, because life typically finds various and surprising ways of turning religious. As Augustine said, our hearts are restless until they rest in God.

In order for our environment and art to be evangelical we must concern ourselves with matters of taste or style. Offending someone's taste may get in the way of an encounter. Resonating with someone's taste may facilitate an encounter. But not everyone or every community will have the same style or the same taste. We will continue to live in this both wonderful and challenging diversity.

Taste varies within a community, through the church year, across a denomination, or across a population. This diversity is unique to our time in history. Through most of history, a population of diverse people would come together in one place to worship and would generally learn a single style, evolve together, or receive relatively uniform style. Today individuals or groups more actively assert their unique identities and don't want it squashed by a colonial mentality or a hierarchical system. They desire to be recognized for their own unique way of doing things. Individual identities are being asserted. Over time some common styles will have to evolve.

Two temptations need to be avoided here: Don't resort to a like-it-or-leave-it approach out of frustration or attempt to reassert one norm. And don't resort to the other short-term solution: "It just doesn't matter. Just do what you want to do." We will need to continue to be in dialogue, seeking to develop common taste within our communities, as well as learning to respect the diversity of tastes we encounter in one another.

Emerging forms of evangelical art for worship: Electronic media arts

The use of electronic media and technology in a worship space presents both opportunities and challenges for the church's worship. Principle S-15

The printing press was a new technology that propelled the reforms of Luther and his followers across Europe. True to that heritage, many Lutheran congregations are using or experimenting with new technologies to produce electronic media as a liturgical art. Like other liturgical arts, electronic media art should be evaluated theologically, pastorally, and aesthetically, and should seek to be both evangelical and formational. The same principles we have been examining apply to this emerging form:

- Primary things must remain primary: Assembly, bath, word, and meal cannot be overshadowed by arts that seek to elaborate or interpret the central things.
- Technology cannot be allowed to drive this or any ministry. The assembly must remain primary. Screens are not places of encounter but the canvas for an art form.
- Electronic liturgical arts must be integrated into the fabric of worship so they are a media *of* worship, like music; not media *in* worship.
- These arts must be evangelical—used to involve extra senses in proclamation or meditation or song or Biblical reflection or to encourage more active participation in the people's work.
- These arts must be formational, shaping the self-understanding of the body of Christ in positive ways.
- Electronic media art can serve a variety of purposes. It can be *homiletical,* supporting the sermon or offering the witness of the laity. It can offer *visual mediations* accompanying a song, canticle, or hymn. It can *foster participation* by offering commentary on the liturgical action or introducing the order of service. It can be a vehicle for *seasonal artistic creations,* inviting meditation or setting the theme of the day. It can bring visual focus and power to *justice issues.*
- Inclusion of this art form in Christian worship, like all the arts, is always a local option and should not be considered "necessary" for the gathering of a worshiping community. Gathering around word, meal, and bath are the only necessary things.

- The needs of the media or art form should never drive the needs of the assembly.
- Balance the use of professional and locally created content. Encourage local participation in telling stories. Balance images, perspectives, and viewpoints.
- Consider matters of justice when balancing the cost of this or any other arts investment.
- Be sure visual artists are fairly credited and compensated. Pay attention to rights and copyright.

———————————————————————

For reflection and discussion

1. Make a list of the ways in which the arts in your congregation proclaim the gospel.
2. Some of our communities approach environment and art with the understanding that, "we will provide only our best for God's house" and others take a more functional approach to appointing a worship space. Discuss the values that each represent.
3. Describe the various tastes or styles operating in your assembly. Are these tastes creating divisions in your community? How are you learning to appreciate one another?
4. How are electronic media arts received in your community?

7
Formational Space: Welcome to Christ

Worship space forms Christians

In the middle of a PBS documentary about his life and work, architect Frank Lloyd Wright says, "Every house is a missionary. Space that is transformative changes the people who live there. Every house is a missionary. I don't build a house without predicting the end of the present social order" (*Frank Lloyd Wright: A Film by Ken Burns and Lynn Novick*, 1998). Of course, Wright is speaking about his vision for the houses he designs for his clients, but what a vision. And what a vision to have for a house of the church: Will our church buildings form us in ways that will bring about the end of the present social order, and usher in the reign of God?

As we consider this place of encounter we must look at how this place forms us as Christians, shapes our encounter, forms our faith. Spaces are containers for symbolic communication, and symbols form people. Art shapes faith, whether or not its intention is to proclaim the gospel.

At the dedication of the Houses of Parliament, Winston Churchill said, "We shape spaces and then they shape us." Walter Huffman, one of the authors of *Where We Worship,* is fond of saying, "The shape of the worship environment will shape the faith of the next generation." I would add that it will shape the faith of this generation, too.

The final section of worship space principles in *Principles for Worship* (principles S-21 through S-25) is concerned with the renewal of worship space and the renewal of the community. This attention to renewal has been the ongoing concern of this book. All the attention we pay to our worship environments, either the existing ones, renewed ones, or new ones, ultimately serves to renew *us*, renew our *faith*, renew our *assemblies*.

The process of building a worship space or reordering existing space is itself an act of faith and worship. Principle S-21

Creating, planning, or commissioning art together forms Christians

It is formative for the assembly to create, plan, or commission incarnational art together. This task builds relationships, teaches the art of listening, of being present with others, treating each other with respect. It's good practice for being the people of God. It is formative. Now, some have pointed out that it is risky. Art is subjective. We don't all like the same thing. Exactly! Use art to discover one other. Build community. We don't have to agree. I know a pastor who uses a collection of portraits of Jesus to get at people's "personal Christs" and their implicit Christologies. Your vision of Christ is different from mine, and Christ is bigger than all of them. Start small. Don't begin with the $25,000 sculpture for above the new altar-table. Start with inexpensive, temporary locally produced environments for the seasons.

Art that transforms Christians invites a relationship

Art that transforms Christians invites us into a relationship—with others, with the artist, with the subject. People long for connections—

with God, with their families, with other Christians, with the salvation story. Formational art can help with that. Lift up artists within the community—as catechists, as part of the formation team. Celebrate artists as leaders. Include artists in the making of new Christians.

Art that forms Christians includes visual arts

Worship has been a multisensory, highly visual experience in the Christian tradition throughout history. Even though the visual arts have almost always had a role in Christian worship, today we live in a visual age. Visual images are now a key component of effective communication. In North America, more than 20 percent of adults are functionally illiterate. Television and computers have driven our culture to an ever-increasing reliance on visual images. Visual experiences are highly valued in our postmodern culture. This generation is more likely to get information from images—television, computers, movies—than books and the printed word. If you're not a visual learner, get someone to help you use visual techniques in educational and formational activities. On the one hand, know that people are bombarded with images all day long. Spend some time creating space away from the bombardment. Use aural and visual silence. Use non-media forms. Use strong, simple, constant images. On the other hand, people are sophisticated and expect excellence in visual stimulus. Bad images will turn people away. Use the wisdom of the church from other visual ages. Remember the way the church in the Middle Ages used stained glass and great works of art, drama, miracle and mystery plays, to teach the faith and guide worshipers.

Art that forms Christians is both temporary and permanent, indigenous and commissioned

Imagine a continuum of the visual arts based on the permanency of the medium. Cut flowers, images on disposable service folders, a mobile, the advent wreath, and electronic media arts are all *temporary* creations serving the liturgy. At the other end of the continuum are *permanent* arts serving the liturgy: the building, sculpture, whatever it is that hangs above or behind your altar-table, and the furnishings in the liturgical center. (A caution here: Don't confuse temporary with flexible. Flexibility is a value we seek in our worship environments. A permanent element of the worship environment, like the ambo, may still be flexible.)

Now imagine another continuum of the visual arts based on their source of origin. Materials created locally, within the congregation, or by members, are *indigenous* arts: bread or wine, quilts, banners, paper pennants, vestments. On the other end of the origin continuum are *commissioned* arts: processional cross, stained glass window, communion ware, or sculpture.

The two continua intersect to create four categories of arts for worship. Seek to balance all these forms of incarnational and formational art in your community:

Temporary indigenous arts

Temporary commissioned arts

Permanent indigenous arts

Permanent commissioned arts

You might take a parish arts inventory by using the exercise found in Appendix A on pp. 85–87.

Art that forms Christians pays attention to all four liturgical centers

The places of the assembly, bath, word, and meal are places not only for encounter, but for formation and re-formation. What is their arrangement? What is their relation to the assembly? To one another? Are they permanent or flexible, or some of each? Are they in creative tension? Or competing tension? What is the progression from one center to another? What do they say by their form?

Art that forms Christians pays attention to the rest of the environment

Formation doesn't happen just in formal settings such as worship and learning. Formation happens in all of life. Pay attention to the artistic opportunities in the space for gathering, for fellowship, for service. Art can be a formative tool in all of life. Examples have been cited throughout the book of opportunities for gathering places, classrooms, and other spaces to intersect with the community's program of liturgical arts.

Art that forms Christians is genuine and authentic

Art that is genuine and authentic doesn't try to be something it is not. It is natural and elemental. If it is temporary and made of paper, it is the best temporary paper art it can be, serving with honor. Seek out simple design, noble beauty, quality materials. Avoid illusion, sham, inauthenticity. Avoid plastic laminate furniture, oil lamps made to look like candles, silk flowers, and spring tube candles that never burn down. Art that forms Christians should convey enduring truths, images, and associations for the assembly. Some paper angels we created once did that somehow. The children made paper pennant angel banners at a Saturday program. The following day, St. Michael and All Angels, these banners surrounded the assembly. The children were suddenly full and active participants in the liturgy, providing an environment for worship, of which they could be proud, and take home after worship. They were a part of it all. And the image of being surrounded by angels was enduring and memorable for the assembly. They talked about that day for two years afterward. Finally, art that is genuine and authentic respects the fullness of the human condition—honestly representing joy and sadness, abundance and loss, faith and doubt, grace and sin.

Art that forms Christians is transformational

Incarnational art draws us out of the ordinary, out of life, and invites us into a new experience. Then it returns us to life, to the ordinary, somehow changed. One pastor in the ELCA video *These Things Matter* says they use art in their congregation to focus on mission, to focus on the world they are called to serve. For the people in the video, the art that invites them into mission allows them to focus on mission, takes them outside of themselves, stretches them, opens them up to the other in a sort of ritual practice or imagining that allows them to reach out more easily later when they are *sent* out, back into the world.

Art that forms Christians transcends cultural assumptions

In *The Use of the Means of Grace* we read: "In these times of deeper contact among cultures, our congregations do well to make respectful and hospitable use of the music, arts, and furnishings of many peoples. The Spirit of God calls people from every nation, all tribes, peoples, and languages to gather around the Gospel of Jesus Christ" (application 11C). The Lutheran World Federation's *Nairobi Statement on Worship and Culture* (1996) identifies four ways worship and culture interact. These points are especially relevant to our use of the arts in worship because all arts emerge from cultural contexts:

- Worship is transcultural. The truth of the gospel speaks to all people, across all cultures.
- Worship is contextual. The truth of the gospel is expressed in culture-specific forms.
- Worship is countercultural. The truth of the gospel challenges cultural assumptions.
- Worship is cross-cultural. The truth of the gospel is expressed in broader ways than the local norms.

Incarnational art is not kitsch

There is a difference between incarnational art and decoration: decoration does not invite transformation or formation. It does not draw us into the mystery. It may or may not be aesthetically pleasing. "Interesting" or "pretty" or "sentimental" or even "aesthetically pleasing" does not make new Christians. Kitsch can be used for decoration. In answer to the question, "What is kitsch," Nancy Chinn offers this definition: "It is fake art. In the church it is the kind of pseudo-art that we often find in religious bookstores. It lives in sentimental bogs of greeting-card verse. It sells itself in clichés. It clothes itself in popularity-of-the-moment, in quick fixes. . . . It is a lie" (*Spaces for Spirit*, pp. 67–68). Never forget—kitsch is formative. In the eyes of some it is malformative. We shape our spaces and then they shape us—for good or ill.

In *Good Taste, Bad Taste, & Christian Taste*, Frank Burch Brown is more generous. In an entire chapter, entitled "Kitsch, Sacred and Profane," Brown reminds us that kitsch is close to the heart. Kitsch in fact has been formational of faith for many people. Being too critical can move us back into the realm of "worship wars" or cultural insensitivity. Our challenge is to help our assemblies seek the greater truth in incarnational art beyond kitsch while meeting many of them where they are. Sounds something like the way Jesus met people, doesn't it?

To avoid the mire, develop procedures that allow for evaluation in the acquisition of the assembly's artworks. This forethought eliminates the hard feelings that arise in both donor and assembly in the event of unwanted but heartfelt gifts. Prepare a wish list for special giving, outlining the congregation's needs and desires in advance. A sample is available on the Augsburg Fortress Web site: www.augsburgfortress.org/specialgiving.

Finally, remember that the goal for art that forms Christians is not to "transport us back to Bibleland." Remember the people's request: we would see Jesus. They come to meet Jesus today, in their lives, not a romanticized, kitschy Jesus that never even existed in the past. Help them meet the Lord today.

Art that forms Christians uses the language of symbols

Formational art allows for multiple access points, depending on one's state of mind, age, background, or experience. This accessibility is important as we come again and again to the same symbol, each time with different experiences and different questions. The parish where I worship practices the adoration of the crucified on Good Friday using a painted crucifix from the Taizé community in France. One may go and stand alone before the cross and place a lighted votive candle there while the assembly sings. This year, for some reason, five-year-old Alex didn't go up with his mom and little sister. He hung behind at the head of the aisle while mom and baby sister went up to pray. When they were done, he picked up one of those votive candles and went to adore the crucified himself, standing there alone in front of the cross. The image and action was simple enough that he could understand it without it being explained, and then enter into it. I'm sure he will repeat a similar action many times during Holy Week in his life and each time he will enter into it with a different understanding.

Formational art is both narrative and metaphorical

Narrative art can teach the Christian story to a biblically illiterate, or postliterate people (remember the stained glass windows). Using art to teach story in a visual society like ours is important. But formational art must also include metaphorical art to balance the narrative. Metaphorical art yokes two apparently unrelated things together, allowing new ways of seeing and enabling transformation. For example, consider Salvador Dali's *Last Supper* (www.columbia.edu/~ef158/supper.jpg), in which Jesus uses American Sign Language to say "Come unto me." All three kinds of sacred space seem to merge, as do time, matter, and light. Here Jesus is portrayed with the clean-shaven virility of youth common among the first images ever made of Christ as a young shepherd.

This early theme of the youthful Christ reinterpreted for our time continues in William Hart McNichols's modern icon of Jesus, "Jesuchristo el lucero radiante del alba" (Jesus Christ Morning Star, www.puffin.creighton.edu/jesuit/andre/radiante.html). Here Jesus appears as a teenage boy, inspired by the tragic loss of life at Columbine High School and the events of September 11, 2001. This figure also brings to my mind the plight of Palestinian youth today, helping me to see again the presence of Christ in our broken world. This young Christ is full of the promise of the future.

As Lutherans, we have a great heritage of using music to transform us, and of honoring musicians and their gifts. In these later days, the work of the artist—local and professional—the architect, designer, carpenter, painter, sculptor, woodcarver, potter, weaver, tailor, dancer, and actor, are important resources in our evangelical tool kit. Honor these artists. Include them as leaders in your assembly. As a people, we have often embraced new technologies and all the arts in our efforts to be faithful to the gospel. As we renew our worship with theological reflection about our use of art and architecture, apply gospel principles to our places of encounter, and find local answers to the question, "How are we gonna get this thing to serve?" we will learn to better use all these gifts in the making and forming of Christians, so that when people come and plead, ". . . we would see Jesus," we can be sure they have every opportunity to meet the risen Lord.

For reflection and discussion

1. How have you used material artists in your congregation in the forming and shaping of Christian faith? Can you imagine any new opportunities after reading this chapter?
2. What effect does mass-produced religious art have on the faith of your assembly?
3. Describe an experience where a piece of art moved you to understand the gospel in a new way.
4. Discuss how nonreligious works might convey religious truths. Are material arts used as sermon illustrations in your congregation? If not, how might they be used authentically in your setting?
5. How do you encourage artists and gifts of art in your community?

Appendix A:
Formational Arts Inventory

With the worship committee, altar guild, building committee, adult forum, or seasonal worship environment group, duplicate the following forms and take an inventory of how well your congregation uses arts of all types. Administer this exercise individually using copies of the worksheets in the book or as a group, reproducing the forms on a large flip chart.

Step 1. Invite each participant to list all the artistic works or activities they can think of that happen in your congregation's worship life (reproducible page 1). Use a wide definition—anything physical, incarnational, formational.

Step 2. When the inventories are complete, in the first column (P), put a mark by every item that is a *permanent* addition to your church building. In the second column (T), put a mark by every item that is *temporary*. In the third column (I), put a mark by every item that is created locally, is *indigenous*, created by a volunteer or nonprofessional artist in the community. Finally, in the last column (C), put a mark by every item that is created by a professional artist (typically *commissioned* or from a retailer, in the parish or not, paid or unpaid).

Step 3. Now, let's transfer this inventory to a grid (reproducible page 2) to see how we are doing in using the breadth of artistic forms available to us. If you identified an item as temporary and indigenous, write it in the upper left quadrant. If you identified an item as permanent and commissioned, write it the lower right quadrant. Repeat for each item on your list.

Step 4. What did you learn? How balanced is your use of the arts? Where are you strong? Where are you thinner? Have a discussion about this balance.

Formational Arts Inventory
Reproducible page 1

ARTWORK, ARTISTIC WORK OR ACTIVITY	T	P	I	C
Example: Seasonal flowers	x		x	

Formational Arts Inventory:
Plotting out the arts in your congregation
Reproducible page 2

Temporary

Indigenous ━━━━━━━━━━━━╋━━━━━━━━━━━━ Commissioned

Permanent

Appendix B:
Resources for improving, renewing, or creating a place of encounter

What makes a worship environment "effective"?

Ask these questions of your worship space or plan:

- Does the space/environment gather graciously and with hospitality?
- Does the space/environment function as a servant of the assembly and of its liturgy?
- Does the space/environment foster and energize the primary action of the assembly as the primary symbol of Christ?
- Do liturgical centers encourage encounter with the mysteries of God?
- Does the space/environment exhibit a sense of sacredness both as house of God and house of the church?
- Does the space/environment reveal Christ? Is it evangelical?
- Does the space/environment form Christians in greater understanding, lead to deeper discipleship?
- Does the space/environment send to mission?

Evaluate theologically, pastorally, and aesthetically

- Is the space/environment theologically sound?
- Is the space/environment pastorally sensitive?
- Is the space/environment aesthetically pleasing?

Process guides and practical helps

- Process guides in *Where We Worship*
  - "Using Existing Worship Space to the Best Advantage," pp. 22–25

- ○ "Renovating, Reordering, or Planning New Worship Space," pp. 26–30
- Appendices in *Re-Pitching the Tent*, pp. 215–245
  - ○ Stages of consultation for reordering
  - ○ Art as an aid to worship
  - ○ Landscaping
  - ○ Appointing an architect or consultant in liturgical space
  - ○ Developing an operational plan
  - ○ Fundraising
  - ○ Installation of new lighting schemes
  - ○ Floor surfaces
  - ○ "The Heritage Trail"—some conservation issues
  - ○ A six-week crash course on the design of liturgical spaces
  - ○ "The Magical Mystery Tour"
- Appendices in *Our Place of Worship*, pp. 71–80
  - ○ Project Specialists' Skills
  - ○ Seven Phases of Process
  - ○ Value and Long-Term Perspective
  - ○ Site and Neighborhood
- Adult study group questions for studying cultural issues (2 sessions) in *Getting Ready for Worship in the Twenty-first Century*, pp. 10–11
- *Architectural Handbook*, Lutheran Church—Missouri Synod (www.lcms.org: enter "architectural handbook" into the search box for a downloadable pdf file)
- Formational arts inventory: see Appendix A, pp. 85–87

Tour and visit

One activity that is mentioned in several of these process guides, and which can involve the whole assembly, is touring and visiting other spaces. Because of the acquired sense of sacredness we have about our own spaces, it is difficult to evaluate them objectively. By first teaching criteria for evaluation and then going out and looking at other spaces, the assembly learns to use and apply those skills to their own space. Visits and tours also allow opportunity to learn about the faith of our neighbor and the diversity of our faith. People usually love to talk about their church building, their congregation, and often their faith. Don't underestimate this important opportunity. Select spaces within your own denomination as well as others. Compare baptismal theology, for example, based on spaces. Select what in your mind are good and bad examples of worship spaces. Use care when critiquing others' spaces based on your values. Sometimes that discussion is best left until returning to your own building.

What typically precipitates environment and art discussions in a congregation?

- Discussions about improving worship space usually begin innocently enough: with the need to replace threadbare or faded carpet, with the desire for a larger font, with the need for improved lighting or a projection screen, with the desire for greater handicapped accessibility, with the need to find a space for the contemporary worship band that is convenient for all. Any of these can grow into a larger and more involved project.
- Alternately, an adult forum can begin to get ideas percolating in people's heads. Look again to the process guides in *Where We Worship*, or simply conduct the class as a six-session study.
- An adult forum could be led using *Principles for Worship*, with the class submitting feedback to the Renewing Worship Web site at the conclusion.
- One pastor/musician team I know used Fortress Press's *The Story of Christian Music* as a yearlong adult forum. The same could be done with Fortress Press's *A Journey into Christian Art* or BBC/Yale's *Seeing Salvation*.

- Or try *this* book out as an adult forum resource (the author would be thrilled to know how it was used).

The renewal of a space for worship is an opportunity for the renewal of a worshiping community. Principle S-25

Resource persons

Congregations, while studying and considering a building or renewal program, are invited to use the extensive consultative services of the church. Congregations are invited to contact these ELCA agencies, indicating the scope and timetable of the projected program:

People with training and experience in creating liturgical space are essential partners in renewed use of existing spaces and in new construction projects. Principle S-23

Mission planning:
ELCA Church Building Consultants
8765 West Higgins Road
Chicago, IL 60631
(800) 638-3522
e-mail for consultants (by synod) at www.elca.org/mif/
    Buildconsultants.html

Building loans:
ELCA Mission Investment Fund
8765 West Higgins Road
Chicago, IL 60631
(800) 638-3522
mif@elca.org
www.elca.org/mif

Architectural or interior design services:
ELCA Art and Design Studio
Worship Interiors and Ecclesiastical Arts
Augsburg Fortress
4141 Station Street
Philadelphia, PA 19127
(800) 348-5887
eccarts@augsburgfortress.org
www.ecclesiasticalarts.org

ELCA Staff Architect:
Peter Norgren
mif@elca.org, or via your synod's building consultant

Guidance in interpretation of worship practice in the ELCA:
ELCA Division for Congregational Ministries
Worship Staff
8765 West Higgins Road
Chicago, IL 60631
(800) 638-3522
worship@elca.org
www.elca.org/dcm/worship/default.asp
www.renewingworship.org

Bibliography

Denominational environment and art documents and publications

Principles for Worship, Renewing Worship, vol. 2. Minneapolis: Augsburg Fortress, 2002.

Architectural Handbook. Standing Committee—Architecture, Lutheran Church Extension Fund, Lutheran Church–Missouri Synod, 1996.

Built of Living Stones: Art, Architecture and Worship. Bishops' Committee on the Liturgy. Washington, DC: National Conference of Catholic Bishops, 2000.

Church for Common Prayer: A Statement on Worship Space for the Episcopal Church, The. New York: Episcopal Church Building Fund, 1994.

Environment and Art in Catholic Worship. Washington, DC: National Conference of Catholic Bishops, 1978.

Our Place of Worship. Ottawa: Canadian Conference of Catholic Bishops, 1999.

For further reading

Bockelman, Karen. *Gathered and Sent: An Introduction to Worship*. Leader guide and participant book. Minneapolis: Augsburg Fortress, 1999.

Brown, Frank Burch. *Good Taste, Bad Taste, & Christian Taste: Aesthetics in Religious Life*. Oxford: Oxford University Press, 2000.

Chinn, Nancy. *Spaces for Spirit: Adorning the Church*. Chicago: Liturgy Training Publications, 1998.

Clowney, Paul, and Tessa Clowney. *Exploring Churches*. Grand Rapids, MI: Eerdmans, 1982.

de Borchgrave, Helen. *A Journey into Christian Art*. Minneapolis: Fortress Press, 1999.

Depré, Judith. *Churches*. New York: HarperCollins, 2001.

Evangelical Lutheran Church in America. *Constitutions, Bylaws, and Continuing Resolutions*, 2003.

Face of Jesus in Art, The. DVD or video. West Long Branch, NJ: Kultur, 2001.

Getting Ready for Worship in the Twenty-first Century. Chicago: Evangelical Lutheran Church in America, 1996.

Giles, Richard. *Re-Pitching the Tent: Reordering the Church Building for Worship and Mission*. Collegeville, MN: The Liturgical Press, 1999.

Hall, Sarah. *The Color of Light: Commissioning Stained Glass for a Church*. Chicago: Liturgy Training Publications, 1999.

Hoffman, Lawrence A. *Sacred Places and the Pilgrimage of Life*. Chicago: Liturgy Training Publications, 1991.

Huffman, Walter C., Ralph R. Van Loon, and S. Anita Stauffer. *Where We Worship*. Participant book and leader guide. Minneapolis: Augsburg Fortress, 1987.

Kolb, Robert, and Timothy J. Wengert, eds. *The Book of Concord*. Minneapolis: Fortress Press, 2000.

Kuehn, Regina. *A Place for Baptism*. Chicago: Liturgy Training Publications, 1992.

Lutheran World Federation. *Nairobi Statement on Worship and Culture*, 1996.

MacGregor, Neil. *Seeing Salvation: Images of Christ in Art.* New Haven, CT: Yale University Press, 2000.

Mauck, Marchita B. *Places for Worship: A Guide to Building and Renovating.* Collegeville, MN: The Liturgical Press, 1995.

————. *Shaping a House for the Church.* Chicago: Liturgy Training Publications, 1990.

Mazar, Peter. *To Crown the Year: Decorating the Church through the Seasons.* Chicago: Liturgy Training Publications, 1995.

Milne, A. A. *The World of Pooh.* New York: E. P. Dutton, 1957.

Occasional Services. Minneapolis: Augsburg Publishing House and Philadelphia: Board of Publication, Lutheran Church in America, 1982.

Philippart, David, ed. *Basket, Basin, Plate and Cup: Vessels in the Liturgy.* Chicago: Liturgy Training Publications, 2001.

————. *Clothed in Glory: Vesting the Church.* Chicago: Liturgy Training Publications, 1997.

Reed, Luther D. *The Lutheran Liturgy.* Philadelphia: Muhlenberg Press, 1947.

————. *Worship.* Philadelphia: Muhlenberg Press, 1959.

Sacrosanctum Concilium, #14, Constitution on the Sacred Liturgy, Second Vatican Council, 1963.

Simpson, James B., and George H. Eatman. *A Treasury of Anglican Art.* New York: Rizzoli, 2002.

Sövik, E. A. *Architecture for Worship.* Minneapolis: Augsburg Publishing House, 1973. OP

Stauffer, S. Anita. *Altar Guild and Sacristy Handbook.* Minneapolis: Augsburg Fortress, 2000.

————. *Re-Examining Baptismal Fonts: Baptismal Space for the Contemporary Church.* Video. Collegeville, MN: The Liturgical Press, 1991.

That All May Worship: An Interfaith Welcome to People with Disabilities. Washington, DC: National Organization on Disability, 1992.

Use of the Means of Grace: A Statement on the Practice of Word and Sacrament, The. Chicago: Evangelical Lutheran Church in America, 1997.

White, James F., and Susan J. White. *Church Architecture: Building and Renovating for Christian Worship.* Akron, OH: OSL Publications (Order of St. Luke), 1998.